Bigfoot Observer's Field Manual

Bigfoot Observer's Field Manual

A practical and easy-to-follow,
step-by-step guide
to your very own
face-to-face
encounter with a legend

Robert W. Morgan

Pine Winds Press

Pine Winds Press
An imprint of Idyll Arbor, Inc.
39129 264th Ave SE, Enumclaw, WA 98022
360-825-7797, www.pinewindspress.com

© 2008 Robert W. Morgan
Cover drawing by Marty Katon
Pine Winds Press Editor: Sand Swenby

Library of Congress Cataloging-in-Publication Data

Morgan, Robert W., 1935-
  Bigfoot observer's field manual / Robert W. Morgan.
     p. cm.
  ISBN 978-0-937663-15-8 (trade paper : alk. paper)
-- ISBN 978-0-937663-16-5 (audio book)
  1. Sasquatch. I. Title.
  QL89.2.S2M67 2008
  001.944--dc22

                                        2008029549

ISBN 978-0-937663-15-8

If you diligently apply the principles described in this manual precisely as they are presented, the trammel veils will lift and the truth will be separated from fiction in this great adventure.

I salute you! Acquiring this manual indicates that you are a special person indeed. I am at your service.

— Robert W. Morgan

Contents

Those Who Dared

"Sure, I've seen a yamprico. Lots of us Indians have. They're what the white man calls Bigfoot or some such. We've got lots of names for them, too, but it always means some kind of wild person who's bigger than us.

Monster, my foot!

"This Apache's too durned old to lie, and too mean to give a hoot what any scientist or religious nut believes. That's the same crew who thought the world was flat and, when they first saw us, they thought they'd got to India. Talk about being ignorant! And, do you think the yampricos give one diddly-darn if those characters believe they exist or not? Those giants don't care, neither do I, and neither should you. Go look for yourself. My adopted son Guynatay [Robert W. Morgan] can show you how."

— *Ciyé Nino Cochise, Tombstone, AZ*

"I've been a hunter all my life. What I saw only yards away from Steve Jones and me was no bear; it was a Bigfoot or, as Robert calls them, a Forest Giant Person. I've seen their tracks and I've heard them too many times to have any doubts. Morgan's methods taught me exactly what to do and what to look for. It worked for me."

— *Glenn Adkins, Louisville, OH*

"I first met Robert W. Morgan when he was a guest on my radio and television shows. While I never disbelieved the stories I'd heard about Bigfoot, I just wasn't totally convinced — that is, until I met this man. He didn't just convince me by talk-

ing; he *showed* them to me on the night of August 30, 1992. Now I'll look anyone straight in the eye — and this includes skeptical scientists with credentials a mile long — and tell them that I've personally seen a living Bigfoot. It was no fake, and he was close enough to touch.

"Working with Robert gave me the most incredible adventure of my life."

— *Steve Jones, Outdoorsman, Atwater, OH*

"Having worked as a professional recording engineer in Hollywood for over 20 years had me thinking that I'd heard nearly every sound that exists. I was wrong. Morgan and I were deep in the woods in southern Ohio one night with no flashlights and no guns. No fakers could have known where we were because it had been a midnight hike taken on impulse — not Morgan's, but my own. He allowed me to choose our destination so there was no chance of my being set up.

"We were alone in a deep ravine that had a creek running through it. The forest was completely around us. As we entered, Morgan gave one of his calls. Damned if we didn't get a response. The further we went, the more calls we received. We realized there were two of them approaching us from separate sides of that creek. Then, everything went dead silent and you could cut the tension with a knife. Without warning, it seemed as if every animal in the world had surrounded us to yell and jabber angrily all at the same time. Morgan and I backed away. It appeared that we had unintentionally fooled those Giants who may have been sentries who expected another band to join them. They were not happy campers. We left. The bottom-line is this: Robert knows what he's talking about."

— *Scott Church, formerly of*
The Enterprise Studios, Los Angeles, CA

"I saw my first Bigfoot while I was out riding my horse near the Ohio-Pennsylvania border. I've seen two giants more since then. They are not bears; it's what we call Windigo. As a Native American of the Seneca Nation, I know they exist — and so does my close friend and spiritual brother, Robert Morgan."

— Victoria Sommers, Seneca Tribe, Poland, OH

"Robert W. Morgan is one of the first persons to seriously investigate and research the mystery known as Sasquatch, or Bigfoot. Robert has spent many years conducting active Bigfoot field research, and he has amassed a considerable amount of knowledge and wisdom, which he presents concisely in the *Bigfoot Observer's Field Manual*. I've been involved in active Bigfoot research for several years and have used the concepts and principles as presented by Robert in the *Bigfoot Observer's Field Manual*. Using his methods, I have had a number of very close Sasquatch encounters as have several members of my research team. If you are serious about researching Bigfoot, you will want this book for your library."

C. Leigh Culver, Atlanta, Georgia

"Since Robert taught me what to look for I've found giant 16" tracks all on my own and I've heard sounds no human that I know could make. It's wonderful to know these wild giant people are out there. I just love it!"

— *Alice Mehaffey, Homeworth, OH*

"Working with Robert erased my initial skepticism. My husband and the others in our team had fallen asleep by the campfire when I noticed Robert pacing about. I joined him for a late night walk along a road bordering a remote valley in southern Ohio. When we reached a point above a narrow valley that held a small creek, we sensed something was walking parallel to us. Being a moonless night, it was too dark to see what it was. Suddenly, we heard incredible slapping and thumping sounds that I cannot explain in any other rational way except it had to be Bigfoot. Then, as Robert taught us what to look for in their handiwork and manually created signs and toys, I began seeing our forests much differently than ever before. Do the Forest Giant People really exist? Well, something highly intelligent is out there, that's for sure."

— *Trisha Adkins, Louisville, OH*

Our Agreement

Yah-ta-hey. Welcome! May I assume that you are interested in Forest Giants and wish to arrange your very own peaceful encounter? I won't tell you that it is easy. Nevertheless, it is possible and even probable — but only if you follow to the letter the systematic suggestions contained within this manual.

Take care, my friend. This journey is not for everyone. It is best taken by special people who wish to contribute something positive toward making our world a better place, not only for the human species, but also for every living thing.

If you choose to proceed, as kindred adventurers you and I must form an immutable bond. If you ask that, I assume that you sincerely wish to stand face-to-face with that wondrous legend some call the Bigfoot or the Sasquatch. In return, you may assume that I can and will share certain things of value that can assist you to achieve that goal.

My sole request is that, in exchange for my counsel, you must promise on your most sacred honor that you will not attempt to kill, capture, harass, or to interfere in any way with the lives and the welfare of these gentle Giants.

Words of caution are in order. To be successful you must remain true to that promise. If you do not, things might not turn out the way you wish — and turn out in ways you cannot imagine. However, by shining the light of good intention into the deepest recesses of your own mind and soul, you may soon be poised to uncover the truth about many, many things — and your life will forever change.

STEP ONE
Where to Begin?

It is critical that you set aside every preconception about where the Forest Giants might or might not be. *From this moment on you must gain your expertise only through your own academic preparation, you must follow it up with hands-on field examinations, and you must never again rely on anyone's research or conclusions other than your own — and that includes mine.*

Don't bother lacing up your hiking boots just yet. I cannot overstress how important this opening phase of your mission is — and if you truly wish to have an encounter, it will involve some serious homework.

Are you up to it? *Good!* So, where do you begin? Start by grabbing a fresh pad of paper and a fistful of sharp pencils and prepare to scour the internet for specific information — *but only for that data which applies directly to your immediate area.* Moreover, do not ignore your local library or that of your community college, university, or the archives of your local newspaper

and your historical society. These can be literal gold-
mines — even though they may not know it. Hints can
be as good as facts if you know how to read them. Also,
do not be deterred by "funny" or "mysterious" encounters described by local news reporters. Remember that
they make their living not by doing all that much on
their own but by reporting events in the lives of others.
Moreover, many newspapers cater to news that enter-
tains rather than stimulates thought. It's that circulation
thing.

Everything begins with that list of reports and how
you analyze them. To be fully prepared for your
encounter you must perform the following seven tasks
precisely. If you overlook a single step, your efforts may
be fruitless.

1. Chart of Reports

Create a Chart of Reports on your pad that has columns for the following: report number, date, time, place
(actual longitude and latitude could prove useful in times
to come), type of event (sight, sound, tracks, etc.), and
your data source. List all incidents — sightings and/or
tracks — that have occurred within an area that is not
more than a 50 to 100 mile radius from your chosen

home base. Why such a short range? The fewer hours you spend driving to and from your study area will translate into more time that you can spend in the field. That doubles or triples your chances for a legitimate encounter. It could become daunting and discouraging if the distance between your home and your study area is too great. In short, be realistic — but don't be intimidated by this limitation. You may be amazed how close you live to these roving bands of gentle Giants.

You will use your Chart of Reports when you later prepare your Master Map. Be sure to arrange the columns on your Chart of Reports in descending order by years, months, days, and, whenever possible, add the approximate times of day.[1] Patterns can emerge from this information, including the seasons of the year. Using a computer, you can easily sort the list in many useful ways: by time, by location, etc. That can be hugely important for what will follow. For example, if multiple reports involving night fishermen emerge in a specific area in October and November between the hours of 1800-2400, this may indicate a habitual movement route

---

[1] I find using military time (0000-2400) is easier than adding AM or PM.

used by night and in the fall of the year. Also, if you have clusters of reports of old legends in that area, this could indicate a long-established migratory route — invaluable intelligence.

Be sure to create a Recent Activity Chart using information from your Chart of Reports that is less than 20 years old, adding time of day if available.

◊ ◊ ◊

Quick story: A grumpy old Viking friend of mine owns a 180-acre farm in a relatively populated area within sight of the city of Alliance, Ohio. He gave me a lot of ribbing when I began researching the areas surrounding his homestead.

"Listen," he snorted, "I was born and raised in this house, and I know every clod of dirt for ten miles in every direction. Even if they exist, there ain't any Bigfoots around here. Go try Pennsylvania!"

After working with me in the field for a short time, probably to escape his cows, both my doubting friend and his charming daughter-in-law simultaneously saw a Forest Giant in broad daylight chasing a deer less than a quarter-mile from his front door. Had they not been aware of this possibility, my farmer friend might have ignored that hulking bipedal form that stood at the edge of the woods watching a frantic deer darting away. Or he would have passed it off as an illusion brought about by sniffing fermented silo juice. My Viking friend is really ticked off now. In the years that have passed since his encounter, he has run into close neighbors who have also seen big hairy people around from time to time but had been too timid to admit it. To add insult to injury, he also learned that his brother-in-law had had encounters outside Louisville, Ohio, only a few miles down the road. No one had the courage to mention these incidents until he broke the ice.

The moral: Set aside all preconceptions about where the Forest Giants might or might not be. If properly prepared, your Chart of Reports will present a solid foundation of intelligence.

2. Further information

Collect further information by researching to exhaustion all available books, magazines, old newspapers, and periodicals while asking librarians to obtain references from the county, state, or federal repository systems. Comb through historical archives for mentions of monsters or haunts, bogeymen, wild men, or *le Loup*

Garou. Above all, don't be shy about bugging local historians and folklorists for their advice. They are deep reservoirs of information and you may find them unusually generous with their time and knowledge once you convince them that you are both serious and appreciative of their efforts. If you truly appreciate them, say so. A smile and a thank you become golden. Also, when you relate these facts to other locals, they will be impressed that you took the time to be so thorough.

Hint: By openly appreciating your professional librarians, they may be more prone to open doors to a wealth of hidden knowledge you may not suspect exists. Properly motivated, these professionals can find out nearly everything about anything. Just make your requests polite and explicit. Later, when you follow up on their suggestions, show them the respect they deserve by saying thank-you with a smile. Ten will get you twenty they will dig even deeper for you.

3. Indian legends

Do not overlook local Indian legends. Become familiar with whatever names that particular tribe gave to the Forest Giant People such as wild men, brush people, shape-shifters, stick Indians, sneakers, etc. If you listen and watch for those names, they could lead you a long way towards your goal. Keep in mind that Native Americans may speak in symbolic terms so that those who should know will hear and those who should not know will never understand. When possible, include this information in your Chart of Reports.

Some of the names used by Indian tribes include:

Yamprico	(Pima/Apache)
D'jenu,	(Micmac)
Kookwis	(Micmac)
Gugwis	(Micmac)
Kiwackwee	(Penobscot)
Windigo	(Iroquois)
Kokotshe	(Cree)
Witigo	(Cree)
Strendoo	(Wyandot)
Misabe	(Cree)
T'cenoo	(Abnaki)
Nikolina	(Koyukuk)
Mahoni	(Yukon tribes)
Sasquatch	(BC Canada)
Ohmah-ah	(Hoopa)
Toonijuk	(Inuit)
Tornit	(Inuit)

Dsonoqua	(Kwakiutl)
Iwashikatchi-nahti	(Seminole)
Sha-wan-nook-chobee	(Miccosukee)
Nakani	(Athabascan)
Matah Kagmi	(Modoc)

Do not be intimidated by myths of Giants stealing children or attacking hikers or campers, or any other horror story you might read.[2] It's nonsense, but with its own purpose. Native Americans use frightening tales to keep their children close to the fire at night, just like you try to keep your kids inside.

On the other hand, there are dozens of tales about Giants that helped lost children and adult humans and at times kept them from harm. I know of a report from 2002, when a college student fell in a Montana wilderness outside Missoula and broke his ankle. He claimed that a Giant had carried him to an active logging road where he was found and taken to a hospital.[3]

---

[2] An exception is the war the New Mexico Cochiti tribe fought with a female giant who had turned cannibal and who was attacking those who were easy prey. However, she was aged, crippled, alone, starving, and could not hunt or forage on her own. See *Soul Snatchers: A Quest for True Human Beings* for details.

[3] As is common in many such incidents, the student demanded anonymity out of fear of ridicule when reporting the experience.

The wisest shamans among the native tribes taught their fellow tribesmen that the Forest Giants must be treated with respect. Certain shamans were known to have formed personal relationships with the Giants that included trading herbs and medicinals, but never food-stuffs or trinkets. The Giants had no interest or need for them. *Think about that.* In some isolated cases, there was a symbolic relationship between tribal holy persons and the Giants that included a type of spiritual trade. Emulating that attitude of respect will expedite your path to success.

Be aware too that it is counterproductive to invade Native American property asking a hundred questions about their "myths and legends." You certainly will be told that no such thing as a Sasquatch or Windigo exists. Those elders among the Native Americans who know of the ancient truths have good reason not to share their sacred knowledge. These sovereign people have been treated brutally and sadistically for daring to worship our Creator in ways that Europeans did not approve. Their chosen ways of life were destroyed and everything they freely shared with Europeans has either been exploited or slaughtered to the brinks of extinction. Be respectful. Leave them in peace.

4. Master Map

Use your Chart of Reports as your source of reference to create a Master Map. This map should be large enough to cover all the potential study areas indicated by the densest clusters of reports occurring within a reasonable radius of your home site.[4] I prefer distances on Master Maps to be expressed in both English and metric measurements.[5] Firmly attach your map to stiff cardboard or plywood and cover it with a clear plastic film thick enough to accept notations using an *erasable* felt-tip pen or grease pencil. Fasten this map to a hook on a wall in the basement, in your bedroom, or behind a door. Store it out of sight when not in active use. There are lockable map cases available; they provide the best security. Even a casual glance could make you vulnerable to pranks from well-meaning friends that could cost you time, money, dignity, and sometimes their friendship.

---

[4] Pay special attention to areas where the clusters are at both ends of a valley or a waterway. These could indicate a travel route. If so, pay extra special attention to the time of day and season.

[5] To convert between English and metric measurements: One meter equals feet times 0.3048. One hundred feet equals 30.48 meters.

Mark the location of each Report on your Master Map's plastic cover with a small x and numerals (1, 2, 3, etc.) to correspond to the items listed on your Chart of Reports, and add identification codes. I use the following, but you should adapt the codes to your particular situation.

- **S** refers to a sighting.
- **T** refers to tracks.
- **ST** refers to both a sighting and tracks.
- **L** means the source was either an early settler's report or an Indian legend.
- **O** is for anything other than the above and you can note that in a margin.

Examples: Your codes might look something like this for Reports 1 through 5.

- **1-S** means report #1 is about a sighting.
- **2-T** means report #2 is about tracks.
- **3-ST** means report #3 is about both a sighting and tracks.
- **4-L** means report #4 refers to a settler's report or Indian legend.
- **5-O** means report #5 describes only screams, hair, etc.

In addition to noting the codes from your Chart of Reports, adding a color code can help you analyze situations at a glance. I use red for sightings, green for tracks, red circled by green for a sighting plus tracks, blue for historical sightings, and yellow for others. You will find clusters emerging on your Master Map. These clusters depend upon two factors: the literal presence of Forest Giants plus the presence of human witnesses. Sightings appear in rashes and are often the result of a human condition that may be "me-too-isms." However, at this point in your work only one report per area needs to be accurate because you are only looking for guidelines.

Maintain strict secrecy as to your exact study area. The only exception to this policy should be when you spend time in the field. Always leave written directions in a <u>sealed</u> envelope at your residence. Advise only your most trusted friend, your family, or your parents that you have taken this precaution. In addition, place an identical <u>sealed</u> envelope in the glove compartment of your motor vehicle. Make yourself safe by being wise.

5. Topographical maps

Practice reading topographical maps and an orienteering manual until you are an expert. It is wise to obtain the best compass and pedometer[6] you can afford. Never risk your life on a pin-on bobble. Make certain, too, that your compass has a rotating ring and adjust it to compensate for the magnetic declination specific to your area. This degree is usually found as a notation on your better maps and should be taken from the center of the sheet.

Word to the wise: Attach your compass to your belt with a strong cord.

Of course, a global positioning system (GPS) is extremely useful, but only as an adjunct to your trusty compass. After all, electronic gizmos depend upon batteries that could go dead without warning. Being familiar with those "old-fashioned" methods is safest.

6. Location Field Maps

Make Location Field Maps for each area showing the thickest cluster of Reports on your Master Map.

---

[6] Used to gauge distances between points of interest accurately for future reference.

Obtain a second set of topographical maps for the areas that show the thickest clusters of incidents. These maps must be of the greatest magnified scale you can find that covers the entire area and must be transportable in a sealed weatherproof carrier.[7] Use the most precise information at hand, even to the hour, minute, and second of the longitude and latitude of these reports, if possible. I cannot overemphasize the importance of this painstaking homework. If necessary, return to the library and obtain Xerox copies of each report that appears within the clusters and any reports that link clusters together. Study every report within five miles in all directions until you know them by heart. Recalculate your entries as if you are looking for a pot of gold.

Now make a list of all your entries that you have organized into a single column by date and time of day. Identify seasonal and time-of-day patterns.

7. Site Survey checklist

The final step before you physically enter your targeted locations is to prepare a Site Survey checklist to

---

[7] I use a case, but a large zip-lock plastic bag would suffice.

determine the possibility or probability of an encounter.[8] Make a fresh survey upon arrival at each promising site. Never over or underestimate what you find! Be stingy almost to the point of pessimism, yet doggedly realistic.

---

[8] Keep blank copies with you for instant field notations.

Sample Site Survey

1.____ Thick willow, brush, or briar patches within 5 miles.

2.____ 20 acres or more of dense forest or brush within 1 mile.

3.____ Dense forest of at least 5 square miles within 10 miles.

4.____ Logging activity past or present within 5 miles.

5.____ Valleys, gulches, or canyons within 10 miles.

6.____ Federal or state forest within 20 miles.

7.____ Sparsely populated mountains or hills within 20 miles.

8.____ Rivers or streams within 10 miles.

9.____ Creeks, bayous, or swamps within 2 miles.

10.____ Sparsely located residences.

11.____ Dairy, beef, truck, or grain farms within 5 miles.

12.____ Indian reservation within 50 miles.

13.____ Stable deer, elk, or moose population.

14.____ Carnivorous predators in residence (cougar, wolf, coyote, bobcat, etc.)

15.____ Moderate-to-abundant fish and small game.

16.____ Sufficient cover to conceal *you* for five days or more.

17.____ You can hike the area unseen on weeknights.

18.____ Black bear are either in residence or could exist here.

19.____ Sightings on site within the past 5 years.

20.____ Sightings within 5 miles 10 or more years ago.

STEP TWO
Scouting on Wheels

I assume that you intend to become a real-life wild-life photographer, so dress like one. A well-designed vest is invaluable and a pair of brush pants or briar chaps might save you from lifelong scars. Be extra smart and never wear shorts in tick or chigger country.

Take along your camera, maps, pertinent reports, your Site Survey forms, a clipboard, and reasonable safety gear. Drive, bicycle, or hike into those areas of activity that you indicated on your Location Field Maps. Be as innocuous as possible when among other hikers or local folks. If asked, I admit that I am conducting a survey for some future wildlife photography — but I avoid telling anyone that my "wildlife" subject happens to be some hairy giant humanoid!

Hint: While conducting your Site Survey, imagine that you are in command of a squad of unarmed US Army Rangers. Your objective is to pass secretly through this area while clandestinely living off the land. However, each of your Rangers averages seven feet tall, weighs 300-350 lbs., their deeply tanned, naked bodies are impervious to cold and to heat, and they have an enzyme in their stomachs that digests the same raw food upon which bears thrive. You must decide how your rangers would hunt for fresh meat once they get bored with veggies. One huge advantage is your squad is trained like baseball pitchers to use stones instead of baseballs. Consider the effect of a two-to-three-pound creek-bed stone hurled by these giants at 75-100 mph. It would instantly kill or stun anything it hit, right?

Ask yourself if sporadic sneak raids could be committed by your imaginary squad and how they might go somewhat unnoticed by that area's farmers or ranchers. To gain insight — do not take my word for any of it — ask those farmers and ranchers if they ever lose an entire cow, calf, pig, piglet, sheep, goat, or perhaps a chicken here and there. Most likely the blame falls upon that area's resident predators, be they cougar, bear, wolf, fox, coyotes, hawks, eagles, wild or feral cats or dogs, or an occasional human poacher. Ask too how much time each farmer or rancher devotes searching for those missing carcasses. Moreover, ask if at harvest time they bother counting the ears of corn they lose, how many apples, peaches, and pears are stripped away each night, or if they climb their weary bones down from a tractor to look for human-like footprints in veggie patches where a dozen or so carrots, tomatoes, beans, or potatoes have been rooted up. I'll wager that such losses are too inconsequential for concern. Besides, if a farmer did report huge barefooted human-like footprints trotting around their fields, area nut cases would invade their lands, their local newspaper would have a field day provoking laughter and derision, and their children would be mocked in the schoolyard. Worse, their bankers might become nervous when they ask for credit for more soybeans, and their family might be drummed out of the church choir.

With this wealth of information, it is wise that you make a fresh appraisal of each area within your range. Remember that you are in charge of keeping your Rangers alive, well, and hidden. Ask yourself why they should be there in the first place. Is it solely because of its available foodstuffs, is it the better terrain for hiding because of the lack of traffic and housing, or is it the relative absence of human activity? If you can't find an immediate and logical answer to fit your squad's requirements, be certain to ask those same questions while you are studying your Master Map. *The answers might not lie exactly where the sighting took place,* but in what *rims* that area.

This is why you must also study in detail the topography and the ecology around all promising sites. If necessary, return to them once you have studied every facet at home — never rush to judgment. Perhaps 20-50 miles to the north is a vast wilderness area, or maybe 10 miles to the south you'll find neat little vegetable farms surrounded by brushy hills that provide good cover for daytime snoozing and nighttime munching. Alternatively, perhaps these sightings took place in a naturally occurring funnel that links one valley to another. Come on, you are in charge! Why in the hell are your troops there? Think like a Ranger commander! Above all, *think for yourself.*[9]

Now you must commence summing up the score for each of your Site Surveys.[10] Remember that each checkmark equals one point. If any site scores below eight, proceed to the next site. If any site scores 10 or more, your chances are increasing. However, when you

---

[9] Never talk to the local farmers, hunters, or residents specifically about the Forest Giants or you will certainly invite interference.

[10] See page 24 for Site Survey sample.

find a site that scores 15 or better, it is time to proceed to Step Three.

◊ ◊ ◊

Story: Despite cruising at 75 mph along Interstate 84 that rims the southern banks of the Columbia River where it serves to separate the states of Washington and Oregon, archaeologist Bob C. and I spotted a markedly strange trail scaling a steep bluff. Due to its deliberate switchback pattern, it was safe to assume it was man-made. The questions then arose: why was it there, who made it, was it still active, and who, if anyone, was using it?

Moreover, my Master Map, Chart of Reports, Recent Activity Chart,[11] and a recent Location Field Map had made me aware that the Forest Giant People routinely circumvented The Dalles, Oregon, both to the east and to the west. I knew pretty well where they crossed the river to the west of the city, but many easterly sightings also had occurred below that vast farming and ranching plateau between Wasco and Blalock. Make no mistake; the mighty Columbia is a tough swim due to its width,

---

[11] See page 12.

its strong currents, and winds that reach near gale force. Therefore, choosing a place to swim across was no easy task. However, I instantly realized this particular area might prove ideal and perhaps could add credence to those more northerly reports I had recorded near the city of Goldendale, Satus Pass, and Mount Adams in Washington.

Upon closer investigation, Bob and I became intrigued when we discovered the carcasses of four cattle and three deer scattered across the 130-acre patch of rocky ground that spread along the base of that steep bluff. Despite a thorough search, not a single skull was located. In North America, only flesh-eating primates, i.e. *Homo sapiens*, habitually remove skulls either to eat the brains or to display as trophies. We also noted multiple tooth scrapings on the bones of both *Bos* and *Cervidae* that measured 3/8"-5/8" in width; these were far too broad to be mere *Rodentia*. Next, we noted that the femurs of one full-grown cow had been literally twisted out of their sockets, one clockwise with a right-handed grasp, and a left-handed grasp had rotated the adjacent femur in a counterclockwise direction. That feat required such immense physical power that it was awesome to contemplate. Lastly, three skeletons revealed cracked and/or broken ribs in the lung area closest to the heart. Each wound resulted from blunt force trauma — and there was no shortage of potential stone missiles lying around. Moreover, we observed no bullet holes in any carcass.

We then collected several strands of coarse hairs from the barbed wire fence separating the bluff area from the eastbound side of the Interstate highway. Obviously, they were not from deer nor did they resemble cow hair. Dodging across the four lanes of that busy highway, we searched the fence along its westbound side that lay nearest the river. Among a jumble of rocks that could easily provide cover from on-coming car and truck headlights after dark, Bob and I collected matching hair samples. Just as important, we noted deep imprints of huge, unshod, humanlike feet, one on either side of that slightly bent fence, as if something — or someone — routinely stepped over it.

Unfortunately, a nearby scientist at a leading university blithely commented that the sample hairs we had sent "...probably came from some long-haired hippie. And, by the way, his hair had been badly bleached out by the sun..." Discouraged but undaunted, I scoured my resource material maps for such data as your own Master

Maps should soon display. I noted there were clusters of new and old sightings both to the south and to the west of that zigzag trail. These clusters increased around the city of The Dalles but disappeared in the wildernesses of the Oregon's Mount Hood National Forest. Looking to the northern shore of the river that marked the border of the State of Washington, I noted sighting clusters worked northward through the Goodnoe Hills, around the city of Goldendale, and up to Satus Pass to fade into the wilderness surrounding Mount Adams and the Yakima Indian Reservation.

Despite that cursory scientific opinion that we had recovered only "sun-bleached hippie hair," I later returned to examine the downstream banks of the Columbia River on its Washington shores. I was elated to find matching hairs clinging to yet another barbed wire fence! My binoculars assured me I was standing approximately one-and-a-half to two miles downstream and opposite the zigzag trail. Therefore, it was logical to assume the owner of all these hairs had swum that river. Moreover, when tested a second time by anthropologist Dr. Grover Krantz, I was assured that the hairs from both sides of that river not only were a match, they were consistent with Hominidae.

Note for future reference: Our initial scientist, regardless of being well respected, had too quickly assumed that some wayward hippie had his hair ripped out by barbed wire on two sides of an interstate highway before he swam across a huge river so he could have the joy of depositing more hairs on its far side. That is ridiculous, yet you can expect it to happen to you, too. It goes with the turf when you dare to fly in the face of the status quo. The lesson is to seek advice but always, always think for yourself!

STEP THREE
Selecting and Equipping
Base Camp Sites

Be safe — not sorry. I don't mean to harp, but before you embark on scouting sorties that take you into the bush, remember to leave in your home or with someone reliable that sealed envelope containing exact information about your intended route and destination. Ask them to respect your privacy unless you do not return or telephone by a specific time. Remember to also place an identical envelope in the glove compartment of your motor vehicle for any law enforcement or rescue group to find. Other than these two precautions, I suggest you keep your mission confidential.

Upon arrival in the immediate area to be scouted, don't jump into the woods from a rolling stop. Instead, take the time to cruise all the roads in the vicinity and in every direction. Carefully check to ensure that all houses, barns, or other structures you see are marked on your Location Field Map. If there are omissions — new logging roads, county lanes, or homesteads — update your maps. You want to know that area as well or better than the locals do.

What do you take on a scouting sortie? I suggest filling a comfortable daypack with:

- Your "best friend" compass.
- Topographical maps of the area.
- GPS unit if available.
- Your Location Field Map.
- Cell phone with an extra battery.
- Digital camera, batteries, and/or a point-and-shoot camera.
- Small roll of brightly colored plastic surveyor's tape.
- Waterproof marker pens.
- Rain slicker or poncho.
- Waterproof matches and fire starters.
- Flashlight with fresh batteries, spare batteries, and an extra bulb.
- Canteen or two of water, Gatorade, etc.
- First aid kit complete with snakebite supplies (anti-venom) if appropriate.
- Bug spray for ticks, fleas, and mosquitoes.
- Loud whistle.
- Small roll (12-18 feet) of parachute cord.

- Sharp pocketknife and sharpening stone.

- Extra set of dry hiking socks.

- Pad of moleskin to cover blisters.

- Aspirin and any medications or hygiene products you might require.

- Toilet paper.

- A few safety pins that can be easily stashed inside your pack or vest.

- A light lunch that suits your taste and purpose.

- Six to ten 40-30-30 meal replacement bars for emergencies.

- Water filtration straw or water purification tablets.

- Small weather-band radio with a fresh battery.

- Bear pepper spray (in bear country).

- Six zip-lock plastic bags.

- Sunscreen.

- Biodegradable soap for poison ivy or poison oak.

- Roll of plastic to cover tracks.

- A journal pad, pens, and pencils.

This basic daypack is intended for eight-hour scouting sorties — but one never knows what can happen off road, right? Of course, you can add whatever might make you comfortable, such as binoculars or a sweatband. Another optional item is a walkie-talkie that has Emergency Channel 9 in areas not served by cellular phones.

About poisonous snakes, lizards, and spiders: In North America, our dangers are few when compared to other parts of the world. There are anti-venom serum kits available for purchase and easily carried for rattlesnakes, copperheads, and water moccasins; mortality is dramatically reduced despite tissue damage. Moreover, there are anti-venom kits for the tropical coral snake and mortality is also rare if you have a kit; luckily, they are not aggressive. Both the Gila monster and the Mexican beaded lizard are venomous and cause severe pain, but there is less mortality if one gets prompt treatment.

The black widow and the brown recluse spiders cause severe pain, weakness, and breathing difficulties, and they may kill small children. There are anti-venom injections available at some hospitals or regional poison centers. Don't worry about tarantulas; their bites might hurt and swell, but they have not been known to kill healthy humans. Scorpion bites hurt like hell and may be deadly among children. There are anti-venoms kits for them, too.

Bottom-line: I carry an anti-venom kit for rattlers when I am way, way out. In all cases, I practice caution and care, i.e. I always vigorously snap out my sleeping bag, shoes or boots, and clothes in areas where snakes, spiders, and scorpions abound. Be aware, be vigilant, and stay cautious at all times. Moreover, it is smart to scout the actual route to the hospital nearest your study area. The last thing you need when you are injured is to pause to ask directions.

What NOT to take

Do not take a rifle, a shotgun, a pistol, or weapons of any kind.[12] If you fear snakes, take a hiking stick. Better yet, make a snake hook.[13] Simply replace the head an old golf club with a steel U-shaped hook curved about 3"-4" in diameter to the shaft. As an added feature, consider welding a 2" steel spur pointing the opposite direction at the junction where the hook joins the club shaft. I found

---

[12] Except in grizzly bear or cougar country and then make sure the weapon you have will actually stop these predators. However, carry it concealed from the Forest Giants. If they spot it, they'll avoid you.

[13] I never use snake grippers. Except in expert hands, one tends to squeeze snakes too tightly, which breaks their fragile ribs and they soon starve to death. Not good.

it useful when a rabid fox attacked me in the Blue Ridge Mountains. If you see a snake, either walk around it or gently move it from your path. Don't kill anything except ticks, flies, or mosquitoes — or rabid animals. You must always project the image of a non-aggressive entity there to observe and to communicate, not to dominate. You NEVER know when the Forest Giants may be observing you! Study the works of Jane Goodall or Dian Fosse for excellent examples on how to introduce yourself to wild primates. Conversely, George Armstrong Custer's manual on approaching the American Indian is a premiere model for certain failure.

Getting Started

Before entering the woods, determine if your vehicle can be safely parked within a mile or two of your planned entry point. If it is over two miles, consider using a bicycle to get to that point of entry. Be sure there is a stand of thick brush somewhere near the point of entry where you can conceal the shuttle bicycle while you are out trekking about. Cache your hiking gear in that same brush, drive to where you intend to park your car, and then pedal or walk back.

Note: Upon entry you must walk perfectly normally; if you are traveling with a partner, talk together in normal yet subdued tones. Never attempt to sneak up on Forest Giants or their sentries will put their band on guard.

Take your time in locating the site for your initial base camp.[14] Your first concern is to locate one that is secure from casual day-hikers. It should also be within 100-200 yards of a natural water source. Forest Giants tend to not only use streams and creeks as highways that conceal passage, but they must bathe and drink, too. Stay at least two miles away from public campsites.

Ask these questions while selecting a campsite:

- Can you make this a minimum impact camp?
- Can a *small* fire be safely and legally built? Avoid any fire that is even an inch over what you truly need. Campfires reflect off foliage, are dead giveaways to other human beings, and may emit sparks that could start a devastating forest fire. Always act responsibly and follow the local rules. I prefer the safety of compact, low-light propane

---

[14] Don't be afraid to change camps as time passes and your experience grows.

lanterns and stoves. If I cook, it is in short bursts using a compact, single-burner propane stove. Conversely, if the conditions are right and I am truly isolated from humans, I may deliberately build a fire that could act as a beacon to curious Forest Giants who might wonder what in hell I am doing way out there.

- Is water close enough to be hauled in a collapsible canvas or plastic bucket to stash as a fire douser?

- I preserve my night vision by using the softer light of a single 9-volt lantern set on dim-dim-dim; I may toss a red handkerchief over it, too.

- Are there trees 100 yards or more away suitable to hang your food bag 12-15 feet above the ground, safe from raccoons and bears?

- Are there rock overhangs nearby that could shelter you in the event of an electrical storm?

- Do not stash any food item with your gear — not even chewing gum. Bears or ground squirrels could make a mess of your gear.

- Are there dry caves, crevices, or a protective overhang nearby where you could safely cache your camping gear for a week or two in waterproof bags?

You don't want to haul your gear in and out every week unless necessary.

- If bats inhabit the caves you discover, don't disturb them. They are valuable to the ecology and eat a whole lot of those mosquitoes you hate. Take care not to stir up any of their guano. The airborne dust can carry debilitating and even deadly diseases. If you elect to store your gear there, carefully protect it from the guano.

- Are there numerous ground squirrels or other rodents in the area? They may carry serious diseases and also attract hungry snakes. If you elect to camp there anyway, don't get angry with the critters — it was your choice and it is, after all, their only home.

- Could you easily exit your camp, especially after dark, in case of a medical emergency?

- Are nearby trees scarred from lightning strikes? If so, choose another spot to camp. Do not use ridges. Lightning could use you as its rod. No matter where you camp, exchange your metal tent support rods for wood or fiberglass and use dense plastic or wooden tent stakes instead of metal.

- Could Forest Giants secretly observe your camp from one or more sides? Good! That's exactly what you want!

- Could Forest Giants secretly visit your camp in your absence? Yes? *That's even better.* You want to make yourself vulnerable — but safe.

Don't settle too permanently at your initial Base Camp site. You may want to move it a few times, as you become familiar with the area.

STEP FOUR
The Art of Research Security

Perhaps we might agree that living life to its fullest includes testing the limits of our physical, emotional, intellectual, and spiritual capacities. As such, is it not reasonable to expect that genuine friends support such efforts even if they are contrary to their private opinions or beliefs? To me, this is what friendship means, and what loving between mates demands. After all, dishonor comes not from falling short of one's goals, for there are no true failures among those who try; it falls only upon those who do not try.

However, human nature being what it is, the moment you undertake research in this or any other field that transcends the mundane, you may find yourself the butt of jokes from the ignorant, the target of pranks from the envious, or the subject of fakery from the fools. Why? Because *you* are daring to rise above the norm, *you* are daring to ask the why of a mystery, and *you* are daring to attempt to find an answer.

By taking on those dares, you automatically hold up a great mirror to those who pretend to be content with the status quo. You may not realize that these sorts of folks secretly hate their reflected images — and blame you for holding up that mirror. Be wise. Secure your long-sought research area from the ignorant, the envious, and the foolish. Don't advertise, discuss, or boast about what you are doing or where or how you are doing it. If you are criticized for not "sharing" your goals and your methods with those who consider themselves your peers, remind them that they are not paying the costs of your midnight oil, your maps, your equipment, your fuel to search out your area, your sore muscles, and your elevated blood pressure from the tension of the unknown. Because they are not, you owe them nothing except a smile and good wishes.

While being aware that there are groups of tightly knit individuals who operate well as a team, I have chosen to avoid contact with most clubs or associations of self-described "Bigfoot Researchers." From what I have observed, most — not all — comprise a minimum of truly motivated and generous individuals who are surrounded by a mixed bag of talkers, braggers, scoffers, liars, fakers, and those who wish to be entertained at the expense of the doers.[15] Worse, they tout their "expeditions" that are either weekend sorties or, at best, a week in the bush. These are certainly not expeditions.

While I have professionally fielded teams as large as a dozen qualified field researchers for 3-7 months on end that were supported by a Science Advisory Board of 17 dedicated scientists in complementary disciplines, I truly work best either alone or with a compact team. My best results came with one or two special persons who are completely in tune with themselves *and* with the heartbeat of nature. It is then that I can wholly concentrate on every bent branch or torn leaf, every owl hoot or birdcall, every stick that breaks or limb that falls, and every intuitive notion that comes over me. Alone, I am the most vulnerable — and that vulnerability makes me all the more aware of my surroundings.

That's precisely the state you need to attain.

Henceforth, this manual will refer to you in the singular. If you have a small team, the same rules apply.

---

[15] To contact a band of proven and sincere doers, try www.trueseekers.org and/or www.aarf-usa.org. There are others, of course, but only through the American Anthropological Research Foundation (AARF) and its affiliates can I be of direct assistance to you in times to come.

Once you have selected your initial site, if necessary, use your shuttle bicycle to stash the gear for your base camp near your entry point. For extended stays, you may want to advise a local farmer or the owner of a nearby gas station, motel, or bait shop that you are an amateur "wildlife photographer looking for some unusual shots." You are not lying, so you can look them straight in the eye. And, if they ask exactly what wildlife, tell them anything that you come across.

Take your time to establish your base camp. Do not struggle to carry overloaded packs. Why be miserable, sweaty, and do all that huff-and-puff stuff? Sure, it may take a few extra hours to shuttle the smaller loads back and forth from your cache, but this is exactly the type of activity that will arouse the curiosity of a Forest Giant. That is why you are there!

Don't you think this activity just might attract their attention? Good!

STEP FIVE
Setting the Stage
for an Encounter

This critical preparation commences with your first trek back to your selected base campsite. Of course, it requires the presence of Forest Giants, seen or unseen — but it is best to act as if they are there. One never knows, so play it safe.

From the get-go, you must make them curious enough to check you out. You also must prove that you are worthy of their trust by having the patience of Job to return to that exact site months on end and on a regular basis.

Choose clothing that fits the occasion and the season. I usually wear Army surplus gear or muted natural colors, not because I think I can sneak up on a Forest Giant but because it allows me to move around near campers during the daylight without being too obvious.

I also camouflage my tent with branches and ground debris to make it less noticeable to hikers. At night when I have my lantern on I'm less concerned that hikers will stumble onto me, yet I keep the light as dim as possible. Trust me, the Forest Giants will know that you are there.

A word about flashlights and that itchy urge to turn on a boom box — sit on it. Keep those flashlights off unless there is an absolute emergency. Don't you think that the Forest Giants know their effects? If they know you have one and you wave it around every time a stick cracks in the night, there is no way they're going to come close to you.

As for the boom box, how can you hear what is going on if your ears are jammed with Pearl Jam? Okay, but what if you get lonely? If you must have music for a little while, I suggest you take along some CDs of George Winston, Kitaro, or perhaps Vivaldi. Don't laugh — this music will not alarm the animals around you, including the Forest Giant People. Truly, if you insist on playing any kind of music, make it classical or chamber music, but still do so in short intervals. Turn it on softly and play it for no more than five minutes at a time. Then turn it off and wait 10 minutes before repeating the cycle. Listen carefully in between.

Personal observation: While I like Willie & Waylon, I never play country and western or rock music in the woods. Check out the camps of hunters — guess what you'll hear. A logical extension for your Forest Giant research may be that "like folks play like music," and you do not want to be classified with rednecks or acid-dropping hunters.

Next, think like a fugitive to enhance your ability to understand and to anticipate the moves of Forest Giants. Mentally, emotionally, and spiritually prepare yourself for your encounter. You must learn to listen to the heartbeat of the true land that is distant and removed from the sense- and mind-numbing cities, towns, and villages. You must learn to hear and sense the unspoken languages of your psychic senses. You must listen to the wisdom of your soul. You will need all of these tools if you ever wish to touch the hand of a legend.

Personally speaking: I learned to approach harmony within the natural universe through many years of applied self-hypnosis and practice of a meditation suggested to me by my Native American mentors and enhanced by Lama T'ziang Rinpoche. Each of us responds to different stimuli and we march to different drummers, so find and use whatever method works for you. You must become able to sense as well as to hear, see, and smell; and you must be able to project messages of calmness and non-violence through a kind and peaceful aura.[16]

I developed a self-hypnosis CD to assist me to hone a keener edge on my observation and perception and you can do the same thing. I listen to it each night before I sleep for at least a month before I enter the woods for any protracted periods of time. While I am in the field, I use it each evening, preferably as the sun goes down. I find that I stay awake much longer, my attention span is more easily focused, my nerves are calm, and each of my six senses is as sharp as a razor. This system can also prepare you to respond calmly and logically to any encounter you might have with a Giant, no matter what the circumstances are.

◊ ◊ ◊

Let's put a smiley face on our picture: Let's imagine that Willie Forest Giant and his lovely bride Wilhelmina are sunning themselves smack-dab in the center of a five-acre briar patch in a wilderness area far away from smelly towns, busy farms, overcrowded campgrounds,

---

[16] You don't believe in auras? Check into Kirlian photography and you'll learn something.

and trails frequented by hikers. Since most little hairless folks enjoy yelling back and forth, avoiding them has not proved difficult. However, on this day they notice something unusual as *you* begin shuttling gear to your secret campsite.

"What ho," Willie murmurs into Wilhelmina's ear. "Didn't that one just huff by here an hour ago? Come to think of it, that's the fifth time today. My, my, the strange things these pale beings do."

Come twilight, Willie and Wilhelmina casually monitor those flickering pinpoints of light clustered at yon public campground where pots and pans are rattling while weary hikers share their adventure tales of that day. This Giant family knows the routine: they'll burn steaks, hotdogs, and burgers, swig beer, and sing goofy songs around a blazing campfire. Come midnight, the majority will be snoring away. No problem! Willie and Wilhelmina know from experience that virtually none will stray from those camps at night; if they do, they are easily traced to and from the potty by their waving flashlights and nervous conversations.

Twilight fades into night. It is now quite safe for Mr. and Mrs. Giant to go about their business of munching roots, nuts, berries, and mounds of veggies from either the forest or the nearest rows of farms. They can also stun fish, frogs, and turtles with stones, or they may even hunt deer, elk, or an occasional cow, goat, or pig in relative peace. After all, the woods from dusk to dawn are entirely their own to do as they wish — what's this???? What's that dim light doing in the middle of their favorite meadow? Both Willie and Wilhelmina have passed this way all their lives and not once has any hairless beings camped *there* before. Hmmm. Perhaps this should be looked into...

"Why, Willie, look at this. That pale little creature is sitting so quietly — it's alone," Mrs. G whispers. "This is too strange. Usually, they travel in gangs."

"Waugh," Willie grunts. "That's that same dink we saw trotting up and down the path as if it couldn't make up its mind to go or to stay. No matter, love." He grins as he scoops up a stone. "Watch this."

Swish, thump.

"Look out, Willie! It's standing up — *freeze so it can't see you*. What if it has one of those shiny sticks that make such a dreadful noise and shoots fire and causes pain?" After several tense moments pass, Mrs. G. shakes her shaggy head in wonder. "No, there's nothing in its hands — it isn't even screeching. Now it... it's holding its empty hands out exactly the way we do. I've *never* seen those creatures do that. How very, very curious…"

Nevertheless, macho Mr. G. is in no mood for a change in routine. That pale person belongs down in the campground with the rest of those nasty creatures. "Okay, kid, let's give it a show," he chuckles. "You bust up a few branches and I'll stomp up and down. It'll haul butt, I'll betcha."

Rattle-rattle, crack-snap, thump-thump-thump.

"Uh-oh, Willie! It's not running. It's still holding out its open hands and it's making sounds at us that are ever so nice — wait a minute! That's the same one we saw a month ago way over the ridge, remember? He didn't run then, either. It's almost as if he knows we are here and he's trying to tell us something. I wonder what that is. Maybe we should…"

"Watch it, love," Willie growls while tugging her away. "They're a tricky lot. If he is still here tomorrow night, maybe we can try something else. I haven't used a good scream in a year."

"What if it doesn't go even then?"

"Either we'll go — or we'll learn to live with it."

Wilhelmina looks back at that frail human who still stands with his arms stretched out, his palms open, and, of all things, a smile on his face. "That one seems so different from all the others. Maybe we can sneak in a little closer to watch it a little more just before dawn."

"I have to admit I wonder what all those gadgets are that he has scattered all around. He certainly doesn't look like the usual camper! Maybe I will go in for a closer look…"

"Goodness sakes! There's another one with him! It-it's a woman! How did she sneak past us? She is doing the same thing! She is standing there with her hands out and she's smiling this way, too! Oh, Willie, maybe they are nice after all. Let them stay a while."

"Bah, humbug! Let's go. I think the corn is about ripe at Farmer John's…"

Cute story, huh? It seems so unlikely — or is it? It only takes three requirements to make it "your" story: 1) the presence of Forest Giants, 2) their curiosity to come back for more, and 3) your earning and keeping their trust by being non-threatening, appearing interesting, and possessing the patience of Job.

STEP SIX
Creating a
Provocative Routine

Your objective from Day One in the field is to become identified by the Forest Giant scouts as a non-threatening presence. You want to appear markedly different from ordinary hikers so you can warrant their tolerance and attract closer investigation. Make routine hikes in the early morning and the early evening. Design your daily hikes to serve three purposes. 1) Break the boredom with healthful exercise while awaiting nightfall, 2) make you completely familiar with your surroundings, and 3) make yourself and your routine familiar to the Forest Giants.

I like to make ever-widening concentric circles around my campsites to discover the most logical direction they might choose for a visit. I am usually wrong, but it keeps me thinking. Behave normally. Do not try to sneak up on the Forest Giants. Walk casually enough to allow your own observations but don't bother trying to sneak around because your actions may remind them of hunters and put them on guard. If your routine seems predictable and safe, they may eventually follow you back to your camp.

Sleep and rest as much as you can during the day because the Forest Giant People are certainly settled in somewhere safe and private for their rest period. Imitate their time schedule so you can move when they move.

Begin setting the stage in your mindset by assuming that you are never alone. Always presume that you are under the scrutiny of those you do not see. Watch for brief flickers of movement out of the corners of your eyes — the Forest Giants seldom move face-on. Never stare too long at any single spot. If you suspect a presence, scan your gaze past that area as if looking at something else. And never point your finger. Grant them the comfort factor of believing they have you fooled.

This is a tough order to follow: do not attempt to trail or track them even if you see them moving away from you. Be patient! Let them come to you in their own time. *They must always believe they are in control.* At night, keep your eyes adjusted to the darkest areas around you and avoid the hypnotic effects of firelight.

You must also invent your unique way to announce your presence and location as you move along — a distinctive set of non-aggressive hoots, yodels, calls, barks, whines, or cries can work wonders. Personally, I clap my hands, whistle, or simply call out my name — I am afraid to sing; they might bean me with a rock!

Words in and of themselves do not matter although those with the softer vowels and consonants may convey a gentler intent; instead, your demeanor speaks more plainly. If there are two or more of you, don't hesitate to converse in normal tones from time to time.

Hint: Choose a single article of clothing such as a distinctive and colorful hat, vest, or fanny pack that you will wear at all times, in or out of camp, to make yourself identifiable at a glance. It need not be a large or cumbersome item; rest assured that the eyesight of a Forest Giant is sharp. Or fasten a single bear bell to your ankle or your walking stick so it jingles when set down.

During these routine hikes, pay strict attention to everything around you. Carefully observe the signs that reveal the existence and the routines of resident wildlife. Be sure to make detailed notes of every event in a written journal: where and when you see, hear, sense, or smell anything unusual or usual. Naturally, should you find fresh scat, tracks, or hair of any animal, be sure they are included. Soon you will notice a predictable pattern emerging that will establish common events in your study area. Begin monitoring your site for obvious changes. Expect lulls in unusual activity from time to time. Don't let it discourage you. The Forest Giants are semi-nomadic, but they appear to revisit favored areas over the course of a season. Weather and circumstance rather than a clock appear to influence these movements. Have patience, and be as persistent as a bill collector.

Don't overlook anything that is uncommon in the natural scheme of things, such as a distinct change in the routines or attitudes of deer or squirrels. If they suddenly get cranky or overly spooked, you should wonder why.

Keep your journal handy to note or sketch anything that may have been fashioned by a five-fingered hand with an opposable thumb. Look for radically twisted or intricately woven branches, twigs, vines, plant stalks, stacks of sticks, stones, or even boulders placed in geo-metric patterns. In particular, note any branch or stick that could not have fallen or been blown in even by high winds.[17] Learn to "read bark" so you can distinguish oak

---

[17] Err on the side of caution. If you can possibly accept it as even remotely natural, do so. Do not fool yourself!

from maple or elm, etc.[18] For example, if dozens of maple and oak branches are neatly stacked around the base of an elm tree, yet the nearest oak or maple is 50 yards away, pay attention! If you find a large limb above a path or trail, placed parallel to the ground, carefully examine your initial intuitive impression. Was your reaction "barring" you from passing under it or did it suggest a change in direction? Think and also feel! If you have a GPS, record these exact positions. If not, make an entry on your Location Field Map after marking the position at the site with a dated and numbered strip of surveyor's tape. Enter that data into your journal.

At home, meticulously transcribe this information onto the plastic overlay of your Master Map, being sure to include times and dates. Use your word processor to track the times and dates of common versus uncommon events.

This lesson is clear: never ignore anything out of laziness. Develop an inquisitive mind and maintain a persistent desire to know what is and what is not normal to your study area. Become efficient in identifying its

---

[18] Until you are expert, carry known samples in baggies. Collect them yourself.

resident animal and bird sounds, both by day and by night. Only if you truly know your environment can you recognize what is normal and what is out of place.

Ponder this: What might appear interesting at a distance to a Forest Giant while also keeping you personally entertained? Your first thought may be nature photography. Think again. That black-and-metal camera always strung around your neck, the one with the long zoom lens, the same one you keep raising to your face, could look too much like a form of firearm to a super-shy Forest Giant. I'll bet most of them have observed the same basic motion among hunters as they lift a weapon to their face before firing. You and I know the difference because we know cameras contain only film or a data card, and we know they can't hurt anyone. But how could a Forest Giant possibly know that? If you must take pictures, seriously consider obtaining one of the smallest digital cameras.

How about honing your sketching or painting skills? Talk about something that may intrigue a Giant — there you sit making none of those obnoxious noises that always seem to blast out from organized campgrounds. Instead, you habitually leave the beaten path to sit quietly amid open meadows with an easel, a palette, and lots of bright paints, pencils, or charcoal sticks. In nice weather, leave your work out overnight. Let the Forest Giants come in safely to view those bright colors and interesting patterns. No matter how crudely you do it, draw or paint yourself standing with open hands before a family of smiling Giants. It doesn't matter what you paint. It doesn't matter how bad it looks, the point is you're doing something outrageously different from usual campers. That's exactly what you want to do.

Here's another great avocation that can serve to attract all manner of wild creatures. Learn to play a recorder or a flute. How about a harmonica? A guitar? A banjo? Or a sweet mandolin? A dulcimer? These are easy instruments to backpack, and you can make all the dumb mistakes you want without anyone plugging their ears. Don't make the mistake of one rank amateur who dragged a full set of rock-band drums into the nice, calm forest, where he proceeded to bip, bap, smack, crack, and bam for hours on end — to no avail, of course.

Consider collecting arrowheads or perhaps plants, herbs, flowers, seeds, and leaves that you can press and catalog in camp for your edification and future enjoyment. If you are in the Sierras, pan for gold. Or how about taking a good birding book and beginning your life list? Be aware there are compact disks available to allow you to become familiar with birdcalls in your area. This activity can serve a dual purpose. I am certain that Forest Giants routinely imitate various bird and animal calls to communicate between themselves — the Native Americans did it for centuries. Become efficient at identifying the resident species' various morning, territorial, and mating calls from their night noises so that you can tell when something is out of place. Consider your reaction if you recognized a call from a species that doesn't exist in your study area. Impossible? Not really.

How about making slides for a microscope? You might consider taking one with you. And you can do all that in your camp with various items — animal hair, plants, scat, insects. Think about it from their point of view. Don't you think those Giants will wonder what in the world you're doing when you pick up natural things, carry them back to camp and then examine them so carefully? They won't know what a microscope is, but they'll know that you spend a lot of quiet time. Wouldn't that intrigue them?

One last suggestion before I leave you to your own imagination. What do you know about the advantages of practicing yoga for your physical, mental, and emotional health? It may be time for you to learn to practice yoga in the woods all by yourself.

◊ ◊ ◊

Story time: After learning of sightings by fishermen of a "skunk ape" in Florida's Estero Bay, my attorney pal Ted Ernst of Key West and I decided to check it out in secret. Come midnight on a moonless Friday night, we drove to a deserted beach on Black Island. We donned full camouflage gear including black-and-green-and-brown greased faces and hands before we skimmed our canoe across the deserted bay. In less than an hour, we had passed between Monkey Joe Key and Charlie Key to angle north. At Starvation Flats we swung east to slip in among the tangled webs of tropical mangroves surrounding Mound Key. Along the eastern horizon was the glow of Bonita Springs; to the northwest slumbered the city of Fort Meyers Beach.

Ted and I set up a tiny "hide" in a dense thicket that crowned one of the several Paleo-Indian mounds of ancient oyster shells. It was not long before something — someone? — came shuffling about in the shallow waters off Stingaree Key. We snaked along parallel to the sounds — I snapped a stick — and the sounds ended in one great splash. Had that someone plunged under-water? Where did they come up for air? Where did they go? Beyond the usual cries of night herons and the clickety-click of scavenging horseshoe crabs, the only sounds were the pounding of our hearts. It was dawn before we dared to nod off; nearing noon we were star-tled awake by a dozen chattering boys as they headed up one trail and down another followed by two grossly overweight Cub Scout leaders. Much to our chagrin, it became clear that our itty-bitty buddies were entrenching for a weekend of camping. We debated making a withdrawal, but decided instead to observe if the Giants — if that was who had been rummaging around — might find these little Cub Scouts a curiosity. We staked out our pubescent bait after darkness had fallen. Fol-lowing dinners of hot dogs and charred marshmallows — why do parents "treat" children to junk food? — the tubbiest Troop Leader decided to tell a horror story.

"Think about it, kids," Mr. Chubbs whispered dra-matically as he stalked along the edge of the light cast by their bonfire. "We're the only ones on this deserted island. We have no telephone, no electricity, no car, and no way home. We're absolooootely cut off from civili-zation and all alllllone. Or are we, really? After all, this island was once the home of — the double-bladed ax-man!"

Through a screen of palmetto leaves, I noticed the puniest Cub Scout squirm closer to his bigger pal as Mr. Chubbs paced ever closer to where we lay hidden.

"But don't be afraid, kids! The double-bladed ax-man has been dead for years. Of course, that's what everyone thinks. However, who knows for sure? After all, no one has actually seen him since he escaped from the old insane asylum that used to be just across the bay at Estero."

That littlest Cub shot a skinny arm above his head and squeaked, "Th-th-th-there's no place like that over there. My Grandma lives there and she s-said s-so!"

"Aaaah, it was that double-bladed ax-man who burned it down after he killed everyone in sight," their leader droned ominously while gorily describing each murder. For exercise — my only reason, of course — I slow-crawled out until I lay flattened less than a yard from the path trod by that waddling storyteller.

"...and the blood-drenched double-bladed ax-man was limping toward the sleeping boy who had dared to come to his island uninvited. Then, as that boy lay dreaming of his mommy and daddy, the ax-man raised his ax up over his head…"

I slipped my fingers through the grass like a five-headed snake. Scant inches more and his bare ankles would be mine — how would Mr. Chubbs explain pooping in his baggy shorts in full view of his entire troop? Just as my hand flexed open for that grab, a soft hoot of a hoarse owl issued from the woods behind me. I froze when Mr. Chubbs twisted around. His foot came scant inches from my nose. Obviously blinded by that blazing firelight and not thinking to look straight down, this purported master of wilderness arts could see nothing amid the darker shadows that surrounded his camp; he could not even spot a fully grown human being stretched out at his feet. I slow-turned to see that "owl" named Ted waving me off. In my heart of hearts, I knew he was right. With regret, I reversed my slow-crawl — until I was only a yard or two from the screening bushes. That's where I stood up before stepping into the black maw of the mangrove swamp. Behind me, I heard yelps and gasps hissing from a dozen little throats. Naturally, the Great Storyteller was sure they had all hallucinated due to his great storytelling skills. Within moments, he was back into his gory story.

That's when I gave in to one hell of a scream.

That Scout camp was deathly quiet that night, but their fire remained gigantic. I enjoyed watching Mr. Chubbs nervously tending it himself.

Unfortunately, our mystery wader did not reappear. Maybe my scream scared him, too.

Ted and I paddled back to the mainland before dawn.

This true story demonstrates that *no one* should yield to theatrics. Perhaps that lost "wader" from the night before had slow-crawled up on us in time to witness my act. I guess I'll never know.

Another Story: In 1972, I led a small three-man expedition into the Mount Saint Helens area in the State of Washington. Our objective was to test my newest probability theories for locating possible travel routes used by Forest Giants. We made camp near the edge of a narrow canyon a few miles above Ape Cave. Each night we were kept awake by loud "kuk-kuk-kuk-kaak-kaak" croaking-barking calls from what we assumed were owls. When we tried to identify those calls as belonging to natives to that area, we drew a blank. My Audubon manual suggested I should be hearing the barred or the great horned owl, the long-eared owl, the great gray owl, or maybe even a lost spotted owl. None of these fit the pattern of our strange calls. Adding to the dilemma was that we all became unusually edgy, but each time we approached the canyon's rim, the "owls" would move away. Mysteriously, the moment we headed back to camp they followed along to scold us with their angry calls.

George Harrison, the Managing Editor for the prestigious *National Wildlife Magazine*,[19] soon joined us. He also drew a blank. Shortly after recording the strange calls, we became distracted when we happened upon what proved to be the first "Bigfoot" tracks discovered in North America through probability calculations[20] as opposed to blind luck or happenstance. Several months passed before I again pursued the identity of those unidentified owl calls. I visited Florida's Corkscrew Swamp Sanctuary with biologist Laymond Hardy to confer with Roger Tory Petersen, a world-renown Audubon birder. Dr. Petersen made identification in a heartbeat, but added it was also impossible that we had heard or recorded such a call in that time of the year. Impossible!

---

[19] Now a Contributing Editor to *Birds & Blooms*.

[20] *National Wildlife Magazine*, 1971, October-November issue.

According to Dr. Petersen — a man I would trust in these matters — those strange croaking-barking-hoots could only belong to the snowy owl; the problem was that species is silent except during their summer mating season — and that occurs on the tundra of the Arctic Circle. Obviously, Dr. Petersen summarily concluded, there had been no breeding snowy owls in the state of Washington during that or any other summer.

The possible solution hit me like a runaway freight train. Anthropologists generally accept that the ancestors to some if not all the Amerindian peoples traversed the Bering Strait Land Bridge that once linked Asia to North America. The sole problem was the date of their arrival. Most findings had limited inhabitation to about 11,000 years ago, which was a bit early to explain findings at Clovis and Blackwater Draw. This cast dissention among anthropologists and archaeologists — which is fine because every theory should be challenged and tested before it is accepted as factual. However, in January 2004, it was announced in a prominent science journal that a 30,000 year-old hunt site had been located along the Yana River, which is situated some 300 miles above the Arctic Circle in Siberia. Paleontologist Donald Grayson of Washington State University felt this was extremely enlightening because it provided the first hard evidence that humans thrived in those same lands that literally linked Asia to North America. Therefore, if migrating humans were hunting food animals such as the mammoth, musk ox, and wild horses in both continents — and these grazing animals required warm enough weather to support grasses and grains to survive — is it not logical that the ancestors of the Himalayan yeti or the Russian Almas could have followed the same route? Certainly, all immigrants large and small would have crossed the tundra during the snowy owl's summer mating season when swarms of lemmings were a plentiful food source. Therefore, is it not also logical these Giants may have added that strange croaking bark to their communications repertoire? Moreover and perhaps extremely revealing, what would this say about the Forest Giant People's ability to hand down these calls through hundreds of generations?

Tawani Wakawa wrote an article for *Many Smokes*, a national Indian publication, describing his Modoc grandfather having encounters with the *Matah Kagmi*, their name for the Forest Giants. One Tibetan name for the yeti is *Metoh Kangmi*. Very similar, don't you think?

Do you now recognize the wisdom of learning the indigenous birdcalls of your study area? Should you identify a Siberian stork in the hollows of West Virginia, it may be your Big Buddy.

One More: One evening, Steve Jones, a close friend and trusted associate, was scouting a thickly wooded area in northeastern Ohio because of a glut of recent Giant sightings. Suddenly, Steve got "that feeling" while listening to several dogs wildly barking and howling in the distance. Something happened then that bordered on the absurd; a single roar of an African lion silenced those dogs. When he related this bizarre event to me, I believed that Steve at least thought he had heard a lion roar. In any case, we began running down our short list of possibilities. We drew blanks until we discovered a strange coincidence. A wild animal breeding farm was in that area and it had lions and tigers and bears — oh, my! This should have offered a quick explanation except for one detail. That breeding farm was five miles from where Steve had been standing. Obviously, a roar could not carry such a long distance through dense woods. However, a second possibility became evident after due consideration. The Forest Giant People are known to be great imitators. Is it not logical that since Giants habitually borrowed sounds that served their purposes, one may have imitated the ferocious sound of a lion? Whatever or whoever roared that day certainly intimidated the dogs — and Steve, too.

STEP SEVEN
Hair, Feces, Smells, Tracks, and Signs

You must learn to remain alert and sharp enough to notice a full or even a partial track left by a Forest Giant, a mound of its fecal matter, or a wisp of its hair. It is bound to happen if you have chosen the correct area, and you must seize each opportunity. Indeed, the searching during the day for viable samples and the detailed effort entailed in making useable slides each evening can serve you well — especially if you make those slides in your camp. Why? Because not only will this absorbing activity keep you busy and wide-awake for hours on end, it also offers the opportunity to monitor the sounds of the woods around you, not to mention making your passive activity attractive to the most curious among the Giants. You will certainly stand apart from the usual humans whom they have observed and that, my friend, is your greatest asset. You are passive, nonviolent, and intriguing because you are so different.

Hair

Some great places to locate hair samples are barbed wire and wooden fences, the rough bark of trees or low-hanging limbs, and those thorny bushes that like to snag your own clothing. Hair follicles can be extremely useful if you have deep enough pockets for DNA analyses.

Why not reduce errors and speed up your analyses by creating your own library of homemade microscope slides for field comparisons of known animal hair including deer, bear, coyote, wolf, rabbit, squirrel, elk, moose, etc.? Why not ask your local zoos, museums, or wild animal shelters to contribute samples of various tail, mane, leg, belly, muzzle, and back hairs when available? Be polite and professional by providing your own plastic bags and a marking pen. Be sure to include domesticated dogs, cats, horses, cows, sheep, and goats or whatever else inhabits your area. Also, tap into the resources of your local high schools or junior colleges by asking science teachers for help in getting the correct tools for the job; they may have an old microscope you could borrow. Edmunds Scientific[21] also provides a great catalog that includes "how-to" books. You may not

---

[21] www.scientificsonline.com

prove to science what our Giant friends are but you can surely determine to your own satisfaction what your hair sample is not.

Feces

Forest Giant feces are difficult to find and seldom recognized by an untrained eye. It is possible that they deliberately defecate in moving waters such as rivers, streams, or creeks or they may bury it.

In any case, analysis of any scat samples that you may find can reveal much about the co-active ecology of the area. However, take special care in handling scat from any source because associated parasites, bacteria, or fungi could infect you. Use disposable gloves, forceps,[22] sturdy zip-lock plastic bags, a quality laboratory-grade facemask or a respirator, and biodegradable antiseptic soap. All this stuff is cheap compared to the value of your health and can be found in most drugstores or hospital supply houses. Be sure to scrub your hands well before preparing food or eating. Be safe, not sorry.

---

[22] I use needle-nosed pliers that double as a useful field pocket tool.

Where could you keep scat before you analyze it? In camp, you might stash your little treasures in a specially dedicated and labeled ice chest — *not* with your food.

Lacking ice, take your sealed samples — I use two separate zip-locked freezer bags, one inside the other — to the closest running water and sink them into a deep pocket in the shade. To facilitate retrieval I put them in a weighted nylon net and tie a length of fishing line to any bush in sight.

Be aware that scat samples deteriorate rapidly and become more dangerous by the hour as the germs inside them multiply. If you intend to take them home for additional analysis, they should be frozen as quickly as possible. If you have no choice but to use the family freezer, do not remove them from their designated cooler chest. Be sure to spray it with alcohol before sealing the lid shut with duct tape. Defrost these samples only when you're ready to go to work. When finished, burn the remains but don't breathe the smoke.

◊ ◊ ◊

Quick Story: John Shelley, a professional map dowser once employed by the US Navy to locate fliers shot down off Vietnam, was also a member of our 17-

member Science Advisory Board. John had suggested that our expedition team should check the banks of a creek that emptied into a nearby reservoir below Mt. Saint Helens in Washington State. I assigned Peter Lipsio to that task, and he was startled to find 2½ gallons of days-old feces. This deposit reposed several yards off a worn game trail on a shelf that was concealed within a pocket of three cedar trees set high above a swift mountain creek. This particular spot would make a US Army Ranger proud. The depositor could remain safe from view while observing anyone approaching from either direction.

We drove that sample some 600 hundred miles round-trip to the laboratory of Drs. Grover S. Krantz and Tracy Blair at Washington State University at Pullman. They quickly noted that its composition included fragments of bone, thus eliminating herbivores such as elk, deer, or moose. Moreover, no black bear is large enough to make such a massive evacuation. This left Ursus horribilis, the grizzly bear, as a possible yet unlikely candidate because they were not known to range that far south in the Cascade Mountains since the early 1900s.

Months later, I telephoned Grover about another matter, and caught him in a rare talkative mood. He stated that after examining the effects of that sample's gastric juices, he had eliminated bears from his list of suspects. Instead, he had found what appeared to be a trace of enzyme that once had occurred in Early Man but had been lost over the ages.

Despite my urging, he refused to make that specific finding public because he felt that it might lend weight to my arguments against killing even a single specimen. Grover desperately needed at least one specimen to provide the scientific proof of their existence, which he thought was required to have them protected by law.[23] Moreover, such a revelation would also crush science's invisible wall of resistance that prevents it from accepting the reality of the Forest Giants.

The findings would also shatter the foundations of many organized religions who claim that Homo sapiens stand alone in the pyramid of the animal kingdom because man alone stands (on two legs). My attitude is this: whatever is, is. I am not concerned about my

---

[23] I had already been instrumental in instigating the world's first ordinance against killing or harming a Forest Giant, which carries a $10,000 fine. It is treated as a "joke" by the present administration because of the heat they took at the hands of an ignorant media.

desires or the needs of any faith[24] that declares us so darned special — I only care about that which is true.

While disagreeing with Grover and others that killing one would solve the problem, I knew in my heart that he was correct from a practical viewpoint. It reminded me of some years before when I had applied for a grant from the National Science Foundation to financially supplement our work. Despite the support of a Science Advisory Board, I was turned down two years in a row by NSF. Angered and confused, I called for help from one of the Board members who worked with the Smithsonian. He took me for a long walk around the Mall to lecture me on why he or I would never get federal backing for this project. What politician or government employee would take the heat for giving public tax money to fund research that would undermine the foundations of the world's major religions to look for a creature more conveniently kept in the mythical category?

Now you know why you and you alone must fund your own research, and be prepared to be attacked by those who fear such revelations. They have a fear of any

---

[24] As defined as something accepted without tangible proof.

truth that attacks their beliefs. Avoid arguments; no one wins.

Tracks[25]

I urge you to develop and depend only upon your own expertise and no one else's. Use what I am sharing with you as a foundation, but you must build your own storehouse of knowledge through experience. That said, I advise you to build a temporary sand or finely raked dirt pit in your backyard or, lacking space, use a park playground or a beach to conduct a few experiments.

The best homemade track pits are 10-16 feet long and 3-4 feet wide and are well shaded to facilitate observations made under a light source you can control. Join 2" x 12" x 8 ft. boards together to create a frame that you can fill with fine sand and dirt. Rake it as smooth as a Zen garden.

Your introductory lesson is simple but important. Remove your shoes and deliberately stroll barefoot through your smooth sand along one side only. Now repeat that process but this time run like hell down the adjacent side. By holding a bright light at different

---

[25] Dr. Grover S. Krantz authored a fine book concerning tracks.

angles — you'll see more clearly at night — you will learn to identify the bits of sand that dribbled as you walked or exploded when you ran. Note too how deeply your living toes flexed to grip and gain traction for each differing speed. Spend all the time necessary on your belly with a magnifying glass to study the varying pressure cracks and ridges that distinguish the two gaits. Pay special attention to the toe-off and the drag marks made by your heels in both instances.

Now perform a second exercise in that sand pit: Measure the width between the centerline of each of your feet as you walk normally. Compare this with the width of your pelvis. Compare these measurements between your friends who are both tall and short. Keeping in mind what you've learned about the relationship between known human tracks and pelvic widths, rake the sand pit smooth again. Now deliberately extend the length *and the width* of your usual stride in the same set of motions. Notice that the sand violently sprays and scatters off at angles — not straight ahead — a direct result of your hopping back and forth to exaggerate width. A faker's tracks will similarly spray and scatter at angles rather than straight ahead when they try to create the impression of a super long stride and a giant pelvis.

These angles of scatter, in addition to the inevitable flexing of toes from gripping to gain speed and to maintain balance, are prime giveaways of fake tracks.

Now try stomping to give the effect of a "deep" track. Note the added explosions of scattered sand all around the track in addition to the usual ones caused by forward motion. These are another giveaway to fakery. Proper and contained toe-offs that include an obviously flexing hallux, squared-off heels, non-exaggerated depth and width, and an in-line gait are the *only* features that can spell G-I-A-N-T.

The next exercise begins by making a third set of normal tracks that are allowed to age in the elements. Go out every single day, rain or shine, for at least two weeks to observe the gradual disintegration of your sample tracks. In between times, practice walking a mile or more over varying terrain near your home and then try to follow your tracks over the following weeks.

Lastly, let us consider those inflexible wooden feet such as those a few loggers used to fool Peter Byrne and Rene Dahinden outside Bossburg, Washington. I would have thought that these assumedly expert trackers would have noticed that those imprints showed none of the flexing, twisting, or gripping that is normal to a live foot, plus the toe-off is a stiff drag. However, after experimenting with your track pit, you should have no trouble spotting this type of fraud.

Becoming familiar with and perhaps cataloging all manner of animal and bird tracks around your study site could be rewarding in many ways. You would find your skills of observation increasing with each visit, your time would rush by much more quickly, and you might become an object of interest to your big hairy neighbors.

I suggest that you obtain a well-illustrated manual dedicated to all manner of North American animal tracks. Note the differences between bear tracks and hominids. The hind paw print of a bear only approximates ours; its largest toes are the three found in the middle of its track rather than our single great toe. The heels of the bear's foot are somewhat pointed while ours are round and the Forest Giant's are rather squarish. Keep in mind that only *Ursus horribilis* — the grizzly bear — grows large enough to come close to a Forest Giant in size. In addition, if the tracks you find truly belong to a grizzly, their long claws will be in evidence, especially in soft dirt or mud.

What I suggest now will anger some folks and they will call me selfish: I recommend that you or your teammates do not report the location of any Forest Giant tracks. Reports and photos prove nothing conclusive to skeptical scientists and your study area could become swamped with sightseers, contaminated by fakers, and invaded by "monster" hunters.

What *do* you do if you find unshod tracks that are huge and humanlike, yet are at a spot where you are confident that no barefoot human has likely trod? Do NOT shout to your companions, if any, or fall to your knees. Instead, stand still and take several deep breaths while using your compass or GPS to note your bearings and position on your hiking map. Do not take even a single step until you are calm enough to see exactly where you are stepping.

Remember, if those tracks are truly fresh, every move you are making could be under scrutiny. Stand stock-still and touch nothing until your mind is focused. No matter how hard your heart is thumping, try to appear nonchalant while ascertaining if the edges around the tracks are crumbled and indistinct. Have loose pebbles, leaves, needles, or other debris fallen into the depressions and do they appear wind-blown, rain-spotted, or has dew collected? If none of the above, are they crisp, clean, and firm? Is water still oozing into the deepest parts? Are tiny particles of dirt still tumbling in? If that is so, stay calm and casual because you may be under scrutiny by the maker of those tracks. They may have decided to lay down a false trail in plain sight to test if you are tracking them and, if they catch you at that, they may avoid you forevermore. How do I know this? — I learned the hard way by making all the errors I am warning you about.

Now is a good time to apply the first rule for deciphering passive or active fakery. If those tracks are too clear and too easily spotted (or if there is only one track with no others to be found anywhere), they are probably fakes. The key to finding the faker is *not* to mention finding them. The egos of those who resort to such chicanery demand recognition, so you can bet that whoever relates some strange reason to entice you back to that same area is the faker. Go with them if you wish, but act totally unaware. Let them lead you to those tracks, but walk right past them. If they "discover" them and call you back — do what you will.

On the other hand, if these impressions appear to be *fresh* tracks of a true Forest Giant, place all that you are carrying down by your feet and stand straight and still. Slowly, slowly, slowly, extend your arms out from your sides until your empty hands are almost parallel to your waist. Spread your fingers wide, position your palms to the front, and slowly pivot in a tight circle. Your open hands will prove to any hidden Forest Giant that you hold no hidden weapons. As you turn, address the woods in a calm and soothing voice. What should you say? Words do not matter. Your tone makes all the difference. When you have completed a full revolution, continue addressing the densest part of the woods while assuming a Forest Giant might be watching every move you make. History has conditioned Giants to expect the worst from humans, especially the white man. However, if they see you acting differently, you have become a unique experience for them. Instead of reacting like most little two-legged hairless creatures in this situation — screeching, yelling, and probably beating feet for city concrete — there you are, hands empty of weapons, making nice sounds.

Wipe from your mind any thought of following those tracks. If their maker spots you, they are certain to interpret this as an act of aggression and they will vanish. *Don't do it.* Indeed, I have been criticized for not following up on a hot sighting or fresh tracks — situations where most Bigfoot hunters set up childish ambushes that never succeed. Yet my methods have gained uncounted passive and active encounters for my friends and me. Above all, you want to pique the Giants' curiosity by acting uncharacteristically. You want to send the message that you are so different that they may be drawn to visit you in your camp.

However, if you can be certain through your studies that those tracks are at least 24-48 hours old, it might be safe to follow them for a few hundred yards to get a glimpse into how they travel. Nevertheless, if you get any sense that you are being watched, break off immediately and pretend to collect mushrooms or flowers in a direction that angles away from their apparent path.

It might seem contradictory if I now tell you there is no likely harm in returning to that spot the following day to make plaster casts of those footprints. After 24 hours have passed, making casts should not alert them to any perceived danger. By the way, if it appears that it might rain in the time between discovery and the castings, there's no harm in covering the tracks with a small sheet of plastic weighed down at the edges with stones.

To make the casts follow the directions on the package for mixing, pouring, and the time to dry. However, you should also embed a few sticks to help reduce fractures. In addition, if the footprints are in fine sand or dust, spray them with a mist of the cheapest purse-sized hair spray that you can find. Alternatively, for the purists, obtain a small spray can of clear shellac from a hardware store. Just remember to layer it in multiple yet thin mists — don't let the force of the spray hit the dust to disfigure the imprint. Use several layers with adequate time to dry in between applications. Don't rush to pour the plaster until you have formed a solid base.

Voila! You have proof of your tracks to have and to hold forevermore.

◊ ◊ ◊

Story One: A few years back, two self-styled "Bigfoot hunters" allowed their egos to exceed good sense. They made the mistake of calling a rugged logger a "dumb hick" for not accepting them as world-traveling, all-knowing experts on the subject of Bigfoot tracks. That same "hick" went home, fired up his jigsaw, and cut two giant feet from some scrap plywood. When the sawdust settled, he nailed those stiff cutouts to a pair of old logging boots and took a leaping run through some fresh snow. The next morning he and all his pals sat back to watch those two "experts" make total asses of themselves on national television by pronouncing the tracks as real as rain. The logger allowed them to bask in the limelight until they were soaked before he lowered the boom. He politely invited the gathered TV crews to film him merrily bounding through the snow with his giant plywood feet. Those two gurus left town and that logger is still laughing.

Story Two: Trusted friends and volunteer scouts[26] for the American Yeti Expedition (AYE) of 1974 summoned AARF field researcher Eliza Moorman and me to an isolated site near Lake Merwin, Washington. As

Figure 1: Matching stride

required by law, they had been acting as 24-hour fire-guards to a burning slash pile of logging debris.

They showed us an unbroken line of 161 Forest Giant tracks impressed in both soft and hard dirt while traversing diverse terrain. These tracks had emerged from a dense forest at the crown of a hill before marching down the center of a fresh log drag. They reached a meadow and made a sweeping arc before disappearing into the running waters of a winding creek. These tracks measured 17½" long and 8" across at the

Figure 2: Morgan and Dr. Krantz at site

ball of the foot. I ripped my britches trying to match the stride on level ground.

Once Eliza and I were convinced these tracks were real, we contacted anthropologist and comparative anatomist Dr. Grover S. Krantz at Washington State University in Pullman. Grover drove over 500 miles round trip to spend a full day of critical analysis before he pronounced them authentic. He assured us these were the longest string of tracks ever verified on the North American continent. This unique experience provided a major breakthrough in my long-term education.

Those tracks had displayed a characteristic that I had noticed before, but had been unable to confirm because all the other tracks I had discovered had been in shorter strings of a dozen or less. This long line of uninterrupted tracks clinched my suspicion that Forest Giants tend to walk with their toes pointed straight ahead instead of splaying to each side, a trait they have in common with modern *Homo sapiens*.

To better illustrate this, visit a beach or a field of newly fallen snow. Observe the tracks left by yourself and others. The majority of humans walk with their toes splayed to the outside; indeed, some overweight persons are prone to leave tracks akin to a duck's waddle.

Figure 3: Observing the tracks

Figure 4: Estimating height

The next lesson gave me a second jolt. Over the several days that Eliza and I had lingered at the site, I had found myself drawn over and over again to a particular segment of tracks located over halfway up the hill and along that log drag. I was puzzled. Why had those tracks abruptly shortened in stride when there had been no significant change in the angle of the slope and no debris that might raise caution?

While absorbed in this mystery, I heard Eliza calling to me from the meadow below but could not see her through the foliage of the surrounding trees. Walking parallel to the trail, I had taken but a few steps when I froze. As a proportionately shorter person, I had arrived at the precise point where the taller Giant would have gained his first clear view of that meadow with its burning slash pile and human fireguards. Obviously, his reaction of surprise and caution was reflected in that shortened stride — I was witnessing evidence of his emotional response through those tracks. What a rush! In addition, that arcing of the footprints in the meadow also made sense — he had cognitively chosen to follow outside the rim of the light cast by that fire to minimize his risk of being seen by the two fireguards.

Story Three: Bob C. and I had been out on our usual midnight cruise among the winding logging roads that web the loneliest parts of the Cascade Mountains southwest of Mount Saint Helens. As was our wont, he manned the spotlight from the jump seat while I drove.[27] Each time we turned a curve, he would scan the areas missed by our sweeping headlights; we also paused wherever water passed beneath or over the road to spotlight its banks for tracks.

It was well after midnight after we crossed over a culvert and caught a glimpse of what appeared to be a Forest Giant (or a large black bear) hunkered down behind a tree on a high bank above the road. We knew that any aggressive motion on our part would chase him (or it) away in a heartbeat, so we coasted to a halt. I exited slowly and walked around in plain view of the headlights to prove I held no weapon. I climbed the embankment a good 20 yards from the Giant's hide to place a small gift in plain sight.[28] Bob and I continued driving to give that Giant (or bear) time to react.

---

[27] I do not recommend doing any of this. This took place very early in my learning curve. Talk about dumb!

[28] Hearing that I was experimenting with sound devices to attract the Giants caused a wave of wild speculations throughout the Bigfoot

We returned shortly after dawn to find my tinkling gift ignored. However, directly behind that hiding tree we discovered the scattered remains of an elk calf and the impressions of heavy buttocks among the pine needle debris. Finding no hair other than elk, we were encouraged to locate huge, bipedal Giant tracks angling straight up the hill in the center of an old log drag. Oddly enough, our culprit made no effort to conceal a route that led to the crown of the hill to enter a grove of standing parent seed trees.[29] I was jubilant to note that those tracks led directly to a huge cedar log. By carefully lifting the bark that sheathed that old log, we discovered evenly spaced compressions that indicated a recent and heavy tread. However, no tracks were discernable

---

research communities, especially between Peter Byrne and Rene Dahinden. Knowing that my degree was in electronics, they had me inventing all sorts of esoteric contraptions. I laughed myself silly — my "secret" device was simply a few sets of cut-glass Chinese wind chimes that cost $3.00 each. They fit the bill because they were wind driven, disposable, and made pleasant and non-challenging sounds — and I hung them where a Giant's footprints would be easily discerned. Although I had zero success, I let the imaginations of the copycats go wild. That said, I would urge you to use your imagination and never be concerned about what others are doing.

[29] These trees are often left in an attempt to naturally reseed logged patches.

beyond the butt end of that tree trunk. It was as if a magic sky-hook had taken our track maker away.

To avoid accidental cluttering, Bob elected to sketch the tracks we had found down at the log drag while I commenced a nose-to-the-ground search. I spent hours crawling in ever-larger concentric circles that began and ended at the end of that damned log. Frustrated and sweating in the heat, I drew blanks and found nothing. Was I blind or just plain stupid? Obviously, more tracks had to be somewhere. We'd followed him up the slope, into the trees, and all along that log before — poof!

It was afternoon before I took a break to fetch some thick coffee and a can of sardines.[30] I paused in my search midway through the arc of my largest circle. I dutifully marked my spot with my kerchief before trudging off in a direct line toward the parked van. My route was yards out from but parallel to that telltale log—then something amiss caught my eye. Unlike its hundreds of neighbors, a single rotting pinecone had been flipped over and its dankest side was turned up to the sun. Lying beside it in a thick bed of old needles was a single compression and a scuffmark. Every bell in my

---

[30] An excellent pocket meal for on the trail; rich in oil and protein.

brain began clanging. Ten yards more and at right angles to that log I discovered a faint string of equally spaced depressions that led directly to the brook some 30-40 yards away. I followed its water flow down to where it entered the culvert beneath the Forest Service road. On the far side, I found twin smudges of drying mud from a soft foot. I did not follow, but I did salute my brilliant but elusive quarry.

I view the complete picture this way: that previous night our retreating Giant deliberately walked up that dusty old log drag, setting down easy-to-follow tracks that would lead to that downed log. However, when he came to its end, that sly fox had backed up on his own tracks. Midway, he had taken a leap onto a thick cushion of ground before padding away toward the nearest source of running water. He knew he could lose us there because we would have to travel its entire length without the eyes of an eagle if we wanted to find him. Brilliant!

I felt a chill run to the tips of my toes. Had he assumed that we might return to follow him? Had he cognitively bought time to escape while I foolishly crawled around in circles? *In short:* had he anticipated our moves?

Yes?

No?

If not, how else can this be explained?

Now you understand why I urge you to never under-estimate their intelligence and their power to reason. Our arrogance gives them one hell of an edge.

Learning to See

What follows are samples taken from approximately 300 photographs in my private collection that I believe may have been made by the Forest Giants as communication signals either to their brethren or for the amusement of their children.

These have never been shared outside my inner circle, despite the fact that most have been in my possession for more than 30 years. One might ask why I kept them secret. It was because there are "spoiler" people in this world who might have imitated these examples to confuse the issue and to stroke their twisted vanities.

However, the time has come for good folks like you to reach out to our giant brethren with open hands and heart. My sole desire is to give you benchmark examples so that you can learn to walk through the forests and swamps with a fresh awareness and a keener eye.

Henceforth, you must learn to take a studied view of your selected study areas. Remember that nature seldom creates debris in structured geometric patterns or right angles. When you do encounter them, take the time to walk around them for supportive evidence that would require a humanlike hand.

In addition, watch for stacks or items of wood, rocks, or leaves that may have been stashed, stacked, or integrated into a logical pattern. For instance, unless a gale wind hits, most branches and leaves fall close to their source. Therefore, if you discover a maple leaf added to a pattern involving mostly oak trees, take the time to locate the closest maple calculate whether the weather or a Forest Giant is the most likely cause.

I hope the following pictures help you to see what is really there.

(A) These rocks were found in a small and secluded creek bed in Central Ohio. There had been water flowing in it the previous week following a downpour. Note that most appear quite naturally placed with the direction of the water flow. Then observe that certain flat rocks are placed contrary to that water flow. Therefore, these had to have been placed their (a) by a hand, and (b) by a thinking brain.

Figure 5: Two views of the rock standing in the creek bed

Figure 6: Rocks placed on fallen trees

Were they messages between bands? Perhaps. But I would lean more to FG children keeping themselves amused.

Note too those rocks placed on the fallen trees that bridge the creek. These had to have been placed by humanlike hands, yet very few humans ever walk this valley.

(B) Most folks familiar with the FGs recognize that they tend to make stacks of branches that are usually found against the bases of trees. I once counted such 38 "tepees" within a single acre of ground.

Figure 7: An example of a tepee.

Figure 8: Trish McAlister examines a classic tepee.

What differentiates hand-placed stacks from natural fallouts? Begin by identifying the species of the "host" tree. Then check every branch and stick in the stack. If the host is an elm but some of the stacked branches are oak or maple, then check the surrounding area. If the immediate vicinity has no oak or maple trees, it's fair to assume they were carried there. Now ask what logical reason a human being would have to bother with such a meaningless task?

Aside from stacks or teepees, take a harder look at the woods around you. Look for geometric patterns and weavings that are out of place. Take your time. Walk slowly and stop frequently. Should you see anything out of place, walk its perimeter several yards out so you get the overall picture. Sometimes getting close too quickly is counterproductive. Above all, don't persuade yourself; let nature and an analytical brain do that. It's better to overlook clues a hundred times than to create them even once.

(C) The delicately entwined twigs make it evident that the Forest Giants observe detail, are artistic, and have the profound ability to use thumb and forefinger to create symbolic objects. What member of the Family Pongidae has that degree of manual dexterity coupled with creative expression and intelligence? None. And what does that leave? Hominidae. You, me ... and them.

Figure 9: Entwined branches

STEP EIGHT
How To Invite a Giant to Tea

To be a gracious host to a Forest Giant you must first design their party with attention to minutiae. Consider your guest's requirements for a safe and friendly atmosphere that has multiple escape routes and unobstructed views. Add to these the absence of loud noises, quick gestures, flash pictures, guns, drop nets, traps, and land mines. Rest assured that your visitor will be a young and adventurous male. With that rare exception of the Patterson-Gimlin film, females are rarely viewed — almost as rarely as are the very young or the elderly.

Your invitation should begin the moment you drive in your first tent peg. However, do not imagine that you will be present in your camp the first few times a Forest Giant may drop by. While the younger Giants are nosy characters, they also have been trained to be ghostly visitors that vanish in a heartbeat. They are curious but they are not thieves. You may not know they have visited in your absence — unless you set your stage with precision.

To begin with — and with good reason — your observation camp must be kept neat and tidy to an extreme. For instance, each time you leave your campsite you must place everything in the most fastidious of manners. Imagine that a Marine drill sergeant may inspect you in your absence. Each time you arise, make it imperative that you fold your sleeping bag in the same spot and at the same angle and place your smoothed pillow exactly on top. Arrange all extra clothing in such a precise manner that if a mouse trots across it, you will know it.[31] Be as fastidious with your backpack, inside and out, plus the precise placement of your cooking and eating utensils, stove, lantern, extra fuel, matches, and everything else down to your toothpicks and dirty socks. Try using felt-tip marker pens to outline each item atop stumps or any camp tables or create a master tablecloth out of plastic. Whatever method you choose, be certain to place everything in the same place each day before you leave and each night before you retire.

Also, set a few nonessential items outside the ring of light cast by your fire or lamp. These must be placed in a

---

[31] If recollection is a problem, try making a diagram for everything and follow it each day.

manner that will alert you to a visit. Forget food items. While some sick or injured Forest Giants have visited trusted Indians for emergency rations, I have yet to investigate a single legitimate report where a Giant scavenged trash, garbage, or leftover Big Macs. They leave these to bears, raccoons, and opossums. Forest Giants are fastidious consumers of food they gather themselves and avoid all edible bait hung out by "Bigfoot hunters" amid their snares, traps, capture nets, and even their spy cameras.[32]

My experience also indicates that Forest Giants never travel alone.[33] Trap, snare, or shoot one and some-one will get hurt. Forest Giants have a long history of wreaking righteous revenge if a member of their band is either wounded or murdered.[34] Unfortunately, any Giant

---

[32] There are a few credible reports that they may accept certain gifts, but only after they have established mutual trust. Usually, that only occurs between them and Native Americans.

[33] To them, "being together" may mean being a mile or two apart.

[34] For instance, review the grisly reports about the Headless Valley of the Nahanni, or Fred Beck's mining crew at Ape Canyon. Fred shot a trusting young Giant in the back only because he and his family had dared to use trails near Fred's mine and paid a few non-threatening visits out of sheer curiosity. The cabin filled with this coward and his fellow miners was attacked before midnight. While huge stones rained down upon its roof, those quaking miners filled their chamber pots with poop, puke, and pee in between firing at

who dares to defend either themselves or their family against human attacks is tagged in the newspapers as a "savage monster."

Strive to make your camp an island of trust. The items you proffer for a Giant's inspection as opposed to consumption should consist of small articles common to all camps. Instead of hiding them to snare your guest, place them in the open *while making certain that any disturbance will be easily detectable*. For instance, place on a stump or a flat rock: a signal mirror, an open case containing aromatic soap or shampoo, an old toothbrush, toothpaste, dental floss, and deodorant, each arranged with their tips defining a curved line that you have etched with the point of your knife or drawn with your marker pen. Inside your tent, you might also use a color-fully dyed feather as a bookmark at a certain page of a magazine whose cover displays a picture of local nature that might catch a Giant's eye. I have anchored such a selected page with a stone and placed everything where it can be easily seen but protected from wind and rain.

---

every sound. Come dawn, they all beat feet for civilization. Fred Beck never returned to Ape Canyon. Note that none of the men was hurt.

What magazine cover might catch the eye of a Giant? I suggest *National Geographic, Birds and Blooms, Nature,* etc. or publications that display illustrations of gorillas, chimpanzees, or orangutans in gentle contact with humans. The images of Jane Goodall and her chimpanzees or of the folks at the Gorilla Foundation working with Koko are ideal. In this manner, you will suggest to your visitor that you are in tune with passive encounters with living beings other than humans.

If you brought along a portable radio or CD player, tune it to a classical music station or load up a CD of Bach or Mozart and let it play *softly* in your absence. Why classical? It is seldom the choice of hunters. In making such an audio contrast, you will create your own unique and melodic trademark with the Forest Giants.

If you are a woman or have a female companion, do not be influenced by that nonsense that the Giants are especially attracted to women during menses. That belief stemmed from ignorant and chauvinistic attempts to keep this a man's work. Would you believe that two well-known researchers regularly raided public rest areas at night in search of freshly soiled feminine napkins to hang out as bait while they skulked nearby with nets and dart guns?

On the contrary, some of the best researchers I had the privilege to work with are women. In general, they are more patient, compassionate, less fearful, more observant of minutiae, and are not as given to bravado and bluster as their male counterparts.

Why go to all this bother about keeping your camp and its atmosphere so spiffy and organized? It is because when you return from your daily sorties you will know without doubt if anyone or anything has paid you a visit. Be diligent; it's the details that count.

Let me dispel some false impressions you may have garnered from the popular media: Forest Giants are not the brutal, bumbling, destructive, and slobbering monsters you see on TV — and they are not thieves. If your camp is trashed, look elsewhere for the culprit. A messy visitor could be a bear, coyote, raccoon, chipmunk, rat, mouse, or a porcupine — and watch out for those thieving blue jays, magpies, crows, and ravens. Once I had to resort to scattering talcum powder around my shaving gear to identify the culprit that kept moving things about. My shiny scissors disappeared in the beak of a raven the same day I discovered its claw prints dancing all about my stuff.

While a Forest Giant may pick up something to examine it, they usually replace it fairly close to its original position. Note the words "fairly close." The time to come alert is when something in your camp has been moved, yet has been replaced only near its original spot. When this occurs, you may assume that you are under observation. React the same as when you find fresh tracks. Put everything down, hold your arms out with open palms, and pivot in a circle as you speak to the woods. Make three complete revolutions before adding one simple act that could prove important to your mission — obviously, the item they chose had caught their attention, and now is the time to offer it to them. Hold it out in open palms and speak softly as you walk to the place where you left other "gift" items. Replace them with that single item of special interest. Make sure you place it in a precise position. Return each morning and evening to inspect it. If it has not been moved, do your offering ritual all over again. Place it in your open palms and make your three revolutions while talking in easy tones. If nothing has happened after a full week, remove it and begin the cycle again.

Hint: If your memory is as short as my own, try either sketching your camp after you have set it up or make a standardized diagram in advance. This is not difficult since you will know before you leave home what you are taking with you. Do your homework and do it right. If you make any changes to make things more convenient, remember to alter the diagram accordingly. That way, if you sense something is amiss, you will not have to rely on memory alone.

Be especially prudent when assessing odors. Forest Giants do not smell like skunks — only skunks smell like skunks. Of course, Giants are expected to exude what we would term rank, wild, and wooly odors in their natural habitat. Yet things appear to change radically when they come closer to civilization. They often smell downright foul. What is the reason for this contradiction? Perhaps the following account will provide the answer.

Quick Story: A family that rented a rural house on property bordering an abandoned railroad right-of-way in Ohio acknowledged they sometimes found huge barefooted, humanlike tracks crossing their dirt lane. They also described the terrible stench that had always triggered frenzied barking by their feisty hound dog. The wife declared that odor reminded her of a clogged septic tank filled with rotting human feces.

Later, when her husband and I toured the property, he revealed the probable source of this odor. The legal owner of that property also owned a septic tank cleaning service and habitually dumped his trucks in the woods behind that rental house.

"Mister Morgan, you're going to laugh at me, but I'll tell you anyway. One night I heard my dog Ruff barking his fool head off out here by the woods, so I went out with my flashlight. When I got close, I saw a big hairy feller get up off the ground and run off. Later that night we had an awful smell came in the windows. It was hot, but we closed them because it stunk so bad. Come morning, I went back to the woods again. Know what I found? That big feller had been rolling right where my landlord had just dumped a ton of human sewage, crap and all. Can you believe that? He was rolling in human poop!"

Over hot coffee, fresh biscuits, and his wife's homemade jam, I shared with them a conversation I had on this subject with Nino Cochise, the grandson of the legendary Apache Chief Cochise and nephew to Geronimo. Nino had pointed out that native hunters routinely masked their human scents to allow them to creep closer to their prey. It was not unusual to also don animal skins and smear them with fresh dung of the species they were stalking. Our Giants undoubtedly have used that trick over thousands of years to approach game — but also to approach their kindred Homo sapiens. I believe this to be a reasonable explanation of the rank odors that are often experienced when a Forest Giant comes to call — it's our own dung.

Now it's time to prepare for your tea party with a Giant guest, so let's review the checklist:

☐ You and I made a mutual agreement about sharing and caring.

☐ You conducted a thorough historical review of your area and made a Master Map.

☐ You surveyed sites and selected the best based on your surveys.

☐ You made an informed selection of your prime site.

☐ You keep your camp secure from the jokers, fakers, and fools.

☐ You have set the stage.

☐ You have created a peaceful and provocative routine.

Ready, set, — go forth to practice patience!

STEP NINE
After Your Perfect Encounter

Following your Perfect Encounter, you may expect that

- You will feel euphoria followed by utter exhaustion.
- Showers will last until the hot water runs out.
- You will have the urge to tell everything to everyone you meet.
- You will have counter-urges to keep it all secret.
- You will relive your encounter in dreams with varying endings.
- You will have a new respect for life in all its forms.
- You will become acutely aware of our insensitivity to animal life.
- Your trust in popular views of history and science will be tested.
- You will feel that if you don't rush back to that special campsite you will lose your new Giant friends forever.

- Some Fundamentalist sects may attack you for preaching evolutionism as opposed to their version of creationism.

- Your boss may not appreciate employing someone who claims to have seen a Bigfoot.

- You may lose your job or a promotion.

- Academia will publicly shun you while proving supportive behind closed doors.

- TV newscasters are seldom fair or sympathetic. I've been known to challenge them to put a pack on their backs and spend a few months with me out in the woods so they can earn the right to criticize.

- The written news media can be worse. In the dozens of articles I have had written about my work, less than a handful were accurate.

Lesson Learned: Dumb me! I once granted twin interviews to popular newspapers that serve the opposite ends of the spectrum of readerships. The first was a telephone interview with Manny Silver of *The Sun*, a popular supermarket tabloid. I had dodged Manny's calls for weeks because I did not want to chance some weird and preposterous slant bring placed on my work. I had visions of giant headlines: "Morgan Fathers Bigfoot Love Child."

However, when Mr. Silver caught up to me, he advised me that he would do a story with or without my input, which left me little choice but to cooperate. However, darned if he didn't win my confidence through his logically sequenced questions. His interview was both pleasant and professionally penetrating. Puzzled but pleased, I gave Sir Silver the best information I could provide, and hoped for the best.

The second interview was to be face-to-face with Dana Milbank,[35] a freshman feature writer for the distinguished *Wall Street Journal*. Dana offered to fly to Ohio to spend a day with me "in the field." He promised rock-solid journalism that would be fair but tough.

My, my! *The Sun* vs. *The Wall Street Journal* with little ol' me in the middle — NOT a position to be envied!

I asked my pal Glenn Adkins to join me for this jaunt. He is a burly kick-the-door-in type of firefighter,

---

[35] Dana T. Milbank is presently a political reporter for *The Washington Post*. He is a graduate of Yale University, where he was a member of Trumbull College, the Progressive Party of the Yale Political Union, and the secret Skull and Bones society.

EMT, and an avid outdoorsman. Initially, Glenn and I planned to take our NYC reporter into a rugged area in southeastern Ohio where we had been seeking evidence of any Forest Giant family's wintering sites. This tour would require that we take a hike through knee-deep snow, dense woods, and around abandoned strip mines that could prove dangerous. It would be slow going in freezing weather, but no big deal if one is prepared. However, we knew there was a problem the instant we met Mr. Milbank at a Hilton Hotel in downtown Canton. Instead of appearing to be either a scientist or an out-doorsman, Dana T. would have made a great model for Eddie Bauer's newest line of outdoor gear for city-boy pretenders. Worse, his stiff new boots were not insulated nor waxed against snow, and his safari-like jacket wouldn't cover his tender bum from freezing winds. Worse, he appeared bewildered when I asked if he carried a compass.

In Dana's defense, he was bright, obviously intelli-gent, personable, and yet blind as a bat to the sign lan-guage of the wilderness. As an honest fellow, he admit-ted he did not view the outdoors with much relish so I asked if his editor hated him.

Over a typical country breakfast at the quaint and popular Walker's Corner Restaurant in downtown Minerva, I was further dismayed to find that nothing in Dana's background gave us the slightest common ground in either science or nature. How was I to talk with him on the subject of cryptoanthropology after learning that his ultimate goal was to cover politics on Capitol Hill? Oy! What could I do with this *cheechako* in 24 hours that would give him an inkling of our work?

The first thing Dana asked to see was my locked map room where I kept my detailed maps spread across the walls. Would he agree to sign the same Confidentiality Agreement I required of every Field Researcher who works directly with me? No? Next question.

Glenn and I huddled after Dana's new boots had squeaked away from the table to spend a penny. We were less than impressed with our city lad. Glenn also pointed at the gathering leaden clouds. It could snow again, it might drop to 10-15°F or less, the snow and the ice could freeze our lad's buns off, or we could lose him down a mineshaft. A headline flashed before my mind's eye: "Morgan Loses Reporter." We agreed to test Dana's mettle for his own protection by taking him on an easier trek. We impulsively chose a known Giant walkway that had a long history of multiple sightings in the records of the Stark County Sheriff's Department,[36] crossing a high ridge just a stone's throw east of where we sat, off old US Route 30.

Despite a brisk winter wind, we three trekked up to a clearing on a hillock canopied by high power lines. We followed the main path that rose to the wooded crown of the ridge. At a fork, Glenn and I spotted something out of place, but our interest mystified Dana. He didn't comprehend what was significant about a wreath of dried *oak* leaves that had been expertly woven (obviously by a dexterous finger and thumb) into a tight bundle and then placed between the uppermost branches of a 6 ft. *maple* sapling. It meant nothing to him when we laboriously pointed out that the closest oak was 50-75 yards away and *downhill*. Dana's response was to shiver and shrug all the while we were explaining that this could not be a naturally occurring event — it would have taken a wind of extraordinary velocity to pick up this cluster of leaves, twirl them about until they were

---

[36] I enjoyed a convenient edge as a native of that area. My closest cousin, a high-ranking officer in that department, introduced me to reliable deputies who had multiple encounters with our big hairy pals.

bundled together, and then blow them up that damned hill only to deposit them on the crown of a small tree.

Frustrated by blank stares, I went on to demonstrate that this wreath comprised three independent twigs wrapped together — from opposing directions. Nature doesn't do things like that, yet a humanoid hand could do in a flash. Between chattering teeth, Dana said he thought it was probably a lost hunter. I was left speech-less so Glenn took over to explain that in times of peril, hunters might leave markers such as orange tape, paper plates, or even beer cans, but none would depend upon the subtleties of leaf identifications. Besides, US Route 30 was in plain view at the base of the hill so there was no danger of getting lost, for chrissake!

Scratch any hope of taking this city boy on the longer trek. We decided to give Dana-boy a comfortable tour in a heated car. Part of that tour was a brief visit to my crotchety old Viking farmer friend who, along with his daughter-in-law, had gained a good look at a Forest Giant. We noted Dana making scribbles only when our Viking made comments about his neighbors teasing that he had been drinking too much silo juice. That resolved us to limit Dana to a late night mini trek into a nearby area that had an intriguing history yet posed no threat of him stumbling down some damned mine shaft.

However, this diversion would be no sham adventure as we had chosen an area where we had recovered reliable yet sporadic evidence of a Giant's passage. I informed Dana as the midnight hour approached that my most trusted local contact Paul Rozich and I had verified two sightings that had occurred less than a mile from where Dana would have his midnight tour. Moreover, Paul and I had discovered twin eight-foot-long beds in a thick bramble patch where it was obvious that one occupant had slept on its back while the other had lain on its side. We had also found the entire intestine of a rabbit at the foot of one bed that had been severed not by a knife but had been pinched apart.[37] Moreover, that gut was still steaming with body heat in the coolness of that autumn morning which meant we were only moments behind the diners. Dana's response to this mini thriller was a yawn.

Dana's boredom transformed into apprehension as the sun disappeared and night's shadows took over. He sat silent when I spun my Volvo onto a narrow lane that

---

[37] This was also recorded, as it happened, on video tape.

dead-ended at the base of another snow-covered hillock. The night was clear and cold enough to make the snow squeak under our boots as we trudged up to and out across a 180-acre cornfield to a wooded area that surrounded a deep ravine. The lights of the town of Alliance reflected off the western sky and the sound of truck wheels whining down US 62 some four miles north gave the illusion that civilization was safely at hand. Like many *cheechakos* who are unfamiliar with the Forest Giants, Dana wrongly assumed we had to be a million miles from any civilization to find the big guys. That's when I advised him that from where we stood I could take a squad of Army Rangers north to Lake Erie or south to the Gulf of Mexico and barely lose sight of woodlands. Moreover, if we traveled at night, skirted the towns, and stayed off the roads, we could do it in total secrecy I had also issued the challenge that if his newspaper put up the expenses, I would prove it to him — then sharp snapping sounds in the woods below us made Glenn and me freeze in mid-stride while Dana barely managed a snow-crunching halt. Moments later, we heard a series of cracks and crunches as if something was treading over brittle wood. Glenn and I were certainly going into those woods for confirmation of who was doing what. Of course, we would back off if we saw the shape of a Giant — but we sure as hell did not want to take Sir Stumblefoot with us.

Dana Milbank was one unhappy camper when we left him alone on the edge of that dark cornfield, but it could have been a disaster to take him into that tangle of trees, thick brambles, and downed logs. Indeed, Glenn and I barely got into the woods before the crunching ceased altogether. To be on the safe side, we stood still as statues, yet nothing more occurred. We decided the best course would be to return the following day to check for tracks. However, our brief pause in the woods may have seemed an eternity to our tight-lipped reporter. He said little when we drove back to the Hilton.

The revenge exacted by our New York City reporter appeared centered on the front page of *The Wall Street Journal* — complete with my picture. Dana's article attempted humor at our expense and was grossly inaccurate. His unsuitability to assimilate, comprehend, and report on this leading-edge science was glaringly apparent. He especially poked fun at the attention we had paid to those oak leaves stuck in that maple sapling — apparently he had no clue about the importance of what was staring him in the face. Dana Milbank and his editors at the famous *Wall Street Journal* didn't give a damn about such details. The quick grins they got from their readers at The Plaza were more important.

Another shock came when Manny Silver's article appeared in *The Sun*. Unlike the article in the famed *Wall Street Journal*, Silver's article was thorough, accurate, and straight as an arrow.

'Nuff said?

◊ ◊ ◊

A final observation: As you proceed in your personal research for untainted truth, you may experience changes in your cognitive values. What was important before an encounter with a Giant may afterwards seem petty and mundane. You may also experience mood swings and lose patience with those nearest to you who choose to expend their own heartbeats worrying about who won what Grammy or Academy Award and who in Hollywood is dating whom. Don't be angry with them. They have chosen not to enter the graduate program in the University of Life — that is their right. However, from your successful encounters you will have acquired every reason to become a contributor to life's true knowledge and, as important, a preserver of life in all its forms.

You can make a huge difference because you are indeed special.

After all, you have joined Those Who Dared.

Yah-ta-hey.

Welcome!

Sources of Wisdom

It is impossible to repay the sacrifices made for my mission by the martyrs Alvin Arens and Victor Zarley, the expertise of the gifted dowser John Shelley, and the courageous Miccosukee Native Americans Victor Osceola and Robert, Donna, Spencer, Bobby, and Louise Tiger. It is as impossible to overestimate the value of the counsels I have received from Lelooska and Tsungani of the Kwakiutl Nation, Chatascatum of the Lummis, Victoria Sommers of the Senecas, and Tenaya Torres Tellez and Nino Cochise of the Chiricahua Apaches. There are also the shaman Round-Bear and the medicine man Ingram Billie of the Miccosukees, the mystic Yaqui Don Francisco, the Tibetan lama T'ziang Rinpoche, the talented mystic musician John Newbern, and all my treasured confidants who elect to keep their identities private. You can read more about many of these folks in *Soul Snatchers: A Quest for True Human Beings,* as published by Pine Winds Press.

This manual would have been impossible without the support of my research associates that include Ted

Ernst, Eliza Moorman, Mike Polesnek, Jim Helbert, Chris Kimball, Richard Van Dyke, Bill Lee, Steve Jones, Joe Decker, Rick Snowden, Robert Purser, Chris Kimball, Richard Van Dyke, Glenn and Trisha Adkins, Scott Greenhill, Alice Matz, Jason Ott, Paul Rozich, and the benefactors Louisa DuPont Carpenter, Caruth Byrd, and Ralph Scott. I also owe a debt of gratitude to the years of input from my science advisors, the explorer and archaeologist Count Pino Turolla, anthropologist and author Carleton S. Coon, S. Dillon Ripley, George Agogino, Grover Krantz, J. Schoneberg Setzer, James Butler, and E. E. Hedblom, MD. In addition, there are Peter Lipsio, Robert Carr, George Shanker, Ellen Jennrich-Coutlee, John Napier, Harold Perkins, Joan Townsend, Len and Mary Aiken, Jim McClarin, George Haas, and others too numerous to mention but are of equal value and influence. Of course, I am eternally indebted to all those hundreds of trusting persons from around the world who shared their advice and encouragement including Norman C. P. Jones, Paul Coward, Joseph Kalk, Jim Kennedy, Kate and Ed Voohees, Catt LaBaigue, Nancy Lawson, my brother Dave, and my cousin Neil Spring.

Obviously, there are not enough thanks in the world to give to Erika, my patient and supportive daughter of a thousand lifetimes, and Alicia Dorey who will forever own a piece of my heart.

When one travels alone, one is apt to see, hear, and feel so much more...

— *Robert W. Morgan*